Also by John Mark Comer

*My Name Is Hope: Anxiety, Depression,
and Life after Melancholy*

*Loveology: God, Love, Marriage, Sex, and the
Never-Ending Story of Male and Female*

Garden City: Work, Rest, and the Art of Being Human

God has a name

by John Mark Comer

ZONDERVAN®

ZONDERVAN

God Has a Name
Copyright © 2017 by John Mark Comer

Requests for information should be addressed to:
Zondervan, *3900 Sparks Dr. SE, Grand Rapids, Michigan 49546*

ISBN 978-0-310-35030-9 (audio)

ISBN 978-0-310-34424-7 (ebook)

Library of Congress Cataloging-in-Publication Data

Names: Comer, John Mark, 1980- author.
Title: God has a name / John Mark Comer.
Description: Grand Rapids, Michigan : Zondervan, [2017] | Includes bibliographical references.
Identifiers: LCCN 2016040702 | ISBN 9780310344209 (softcover)
Subjects: LCSH: God—Name—Biblical teaching.
Classification: LCC BT180.N2 C66 2017 | DCC 231—dc23 LC record available at https://lcnn.loc.gov/2016040702

Published in association with Yates & Yates, www.yates2.com.

Design: *Ryan Wesley Peterson*
Author photo: *Ryan Garber*

First Printing January 2017 / Printed in the United States of America

24 25 26 27 28 LBC 23 22 21 20 19

John Mark Comer's *God Has a Name* is not just a book; it's an experience. This book is more than just a nutritious delicacy; it's an aesthetic experience full of passion and power, truth and imagination. He's one of the few Christian writers who makes me want to read more (good) books and watch less Netflix.

Dr. Preston Sprinkle, *New York Times* bestselling author and president of The Center for Faith, Sexuality, and Gender

John Mark Comer is a master communicator. More important, he loves the Bible, listens to the Bible, and has learned from the Bible so deeply that what he teaches and preaches is soaked in the Bible. For that reason alone, John Mark has become an important voice in the American church. In *God Has a Name*, we are treated to nothing less than a panorama of the Bible's understanding of God on the basis of one of the most important—and often neglected—passages in the whole Bible. This book will bless your life because it will lead you straight to God!

Scot McKnight, PhD, Julius R. Mantey professor of New Testament at Northern Seminary

The best way to describe *God Has a Name* is if A. W. Tozer's *The Knowledge of the Holy* and Rob Bell's *What We Talk About When We Talk About God* had a love child who rebelled against her parents.

David Lomas, lead pastor of Reality San Francisco and author of *The Truest Thing about You*

In an age when everyone thinks Jesus is on *their* team, baptizing *their* agenda, getting behind *their* ideologies, we have become a people orthodox unto ourselves. "I am the measure of truth," everyone seems to be saying, "and dissenters are to be burned at the stake." By the pen of John Mark Comer, we have a book that will pop our bubbles of arrogance. In the end, it provokes us out of our self-aggrandizement and beckons us into the throne room of worship. Recommended without reservation!

Dr. A. J. Swoboda, pastor, professor, and author of *The Dusty Ones*

Using his unique voice, wonderfully disarming humor, and knack for theological paraphrase, John Mark Comer has crafted another challenging work that we pray will impact readers as significantly as it has our community in Portland.

The elders of Bridgetown Church

John Mark Comer is a wise and stimulating guide who points out just how much we've underestimated the endless mercy of God in the Old Testament. Prepare to have your deepest assumptions about God's character challenged in the best possible way.

Dr. Tim Mackie, co-creator of The Bible Project

"What is God like?" is *the* question one must answer. The Bible itself quotes Exodus 34v6–7 constantly. John Mark Comer's contemplations will assist you to ponder what it teaches. Your mind, spirit, and heart will be transformed.

> **Gerry Breshears, PhD,** professor of theology at Western Seminary, Portland

Across the Western world, there is a growing band of neighborhoods, cities, and towns that hold tightly to their progressive identities, resisting and rejecting Christianity as, at best, passé and, at worst, oppressive. John Mark Comer pastors from such a city—Portland—encouraging us to live a faithful, deep, and devoted life of discipleship. His is an important voice, one that helps us flourish as followers of Christ in contexts in which even the name of God is contested.

> **Mark Sayers,** senior pastor of Red Church in Melbourne, Australia, and author of *Disappearing Church* and *Strange Days*

Despite the growing popularity of atheism, the vast majority of people say they still believe in God. But this "God" is often just a projection of their own values, morals, and ideas. This book is a simple yet profound guide to what God has said about himself. Who *he* says he is. And his true identity and character are both far different and far better than we could ever imagine.

> **Skye Jethani,** author of *With* and former editor at *Christianity Today*

There aren't many questions in life that if you find the answer to them, it can change everything. But asking who God is and what is he like are two of those questions, and John Mark Comer brilliantly answers them in this book.

Jefferson Bethke, author of *It's Not What You Think*

After the first few pages of *God Has a Name*, I threw both fists in the air. After the third chapter, I felt like chest bumping everyone in the coffee shop. By the end of the book, I was Jack Black in the end credits of *School of Rock*. This book is electrifying! I'm not sure who will find this book more earthshaking—the jaded skeptic or the longtime religious! Either way, get this book.

Evan Wickham, artist, worship leader, and church planter, San Diego, California

If you enjoy the read, please tell your friends.

#godhasaname

The path

Note to the reader:

Like most English translations of the Bible, the NIV translates the Hebrew name for God, "Yahweh," into English as the title "the LORD." For reasons that will become clear as you read, we added Yahweh in brackets. Each time you read it, remember that God has a name.

Exodus 34v4-7

So Moses chiseled out two stone tablets like the first ones and went up Mount Sinai early in the morning, as the LORD [Yahweh] had commanded him; and he carried the two stone tablets in his hands. Then the LORD [Yahweh] came down in the cloud and stood there with him and proclaimed his name, the LORD [Yahweh]. And he passed in front of Moses, proclaiming, "The LORD [Yahweh], the LORD [Yahweh], the compassionate and gracious God, slow to anger, abounding in love and faithfulness, maintaining love to thousands,

and forgiving wicked-
ness, rebellion and sin.
Yet he does not leave
the guilty unpunished;
he punishes the chil-
dren and their children
for the sin of the par-
ents to the third and
fourth generation."

Prologue

The God on top
of the mountain

Last week, an atheist came up to me and asked how I could believe in a God who made parents eat their children.

Naturally, I was a little confused. A lot of people have odd ideas about God, but *cannibalism*? That was new.

I was speaking at an event, and the theme that weekend was the Bible—in all its weirdness and mystery and drama and truth and lies and violence and nonviolence and sarcastic donkeys and dying Messiahs and what-in-the-world-is-up-with-*this* story-ness.

The event was supposed to be for pastors and church leader types, but a number of atheists crashed the party.

It turns out a lot of people have issues with the Bible.

Even more of us have issues with God.

So this guy, Micah, comes up to me with a quote from *Leviticus*. (Why is it always *Leviticus*?) He had accidentally torn a line out of context and misread it. It happens.

We had a nice chat about how God isn't actually a cannibal, and then I had to go up on stage and teach. But it struck me later that Micah the atheist and myself the pastor were both talking about God, but the two of us had radically different ideas about *who God is*.

For me, God is the Creator of all that is good, beautiful, and true—the God I read about in the Scriptures and then see in Jesus of Nazareth.

For Micah, God is a sadistic monster who made ancient Hebrews eat their young.

Same Bible, *very different* God.

Then a few weeks back, my son Jude asked me about the resurrection of Jesus. He wanted to know if Jesus was a zombie, like in *World War Z*.

Jesus zombie?[1]

We act like the English word "God" is a common denominator, but it's not.

When we talk about God, it turns out we're all over the map.

In the West, we still live in a hangover from our Christianized past. There was a time when you could say "God," and people would immediately think of the God we read about in the Scriptures and see in Jesus. Most people would even come to the same basic conclusions about this God.

That time has long since gone the way of the earth.

Today, when I say "God," you might think any number of things, depending on your country of birth, language, religion, church experience, background—and, of course, whether or not you have cable.

All of this brings me to the question at the heart of this book: **Who is God?**

I'm not writing this book to prove that God exists. If you're an atheist like my new friend Micah, welcome to the table. We're glad you're here. Just know that I won't go into a litany of reasons that I'm right and you're wrong. There are a lot of people *way* smarter than me—the kind with extra letters after their name—who've already had a crack at that.

I can only speak out of my own life, and, for me, God's existence was never the question. I've been down the road of doubt, had a crisis of faith—a few actually—thought long and hard about Jesus, and had a list of questions about the Bible stretching to Florida and back (I live in Portland—it's a long trek). But for me, the question was never whether God exists. The way I'm wired, that was axiomatic and self-evident.

Have you been outside recently?

For me, the far more interesting question was always, "What in the world is God *like*?"

Is God a he?

Or a she?

Come on, sisters . . .

Is God a they?

Or an it?

Is the tree in my front yard full of the divine?

Am I?

Is God even a person? Or is he/she/they/it/the tree/maybe-even-me more of an energy force or a state of mind?

Or is Micah right? Is God just a myth? A carryover from a world that all smart, thinking people have moved on from? Now that we have science and technology, "we know better."

Let's assume for now that there *is* some kind of an invisible-but-real being who made everything, and for now let's call this being "God." If so, what is this God *like*?

Kind, or cruel?

Close by and involved in my life, or far-off and aloof?

Strict and uptight like a fundamentalist preacher, or free and easygoing like a good, educated progressive?

Does he vote Democratic? Or is he a Republican? Maybe Green Party?

Or how about this one: Is God even good for the world anymore? Fewer and fewer people answer yes. What if God and religion are just an endless source of violence and hatred and bigotry and hypocrisy and really bad music?

Who is this "God" we love, hate, worship, blaspheme, trust, fear, believe in, doubt, cuss in the name of, bow to, make jokes about, and most of the time just ignore?

I would argue that how you answer this question will *define* you.

The twentieth-century writer A. W. Tozer made a stunning claim: "What comes into our minds when we think about God is the most important thing about us."[2]

Really?

The most important thing?

More than our gender or sexuality or ethnicity or family of origin or the town we grew up in or where we went to college or our tax bracket or whether our sport is American football or *futbol* football?

Absolutely.

Here's a truth that cuts across the whole of the universe: **we become like what we worship**.

Tozer went on to write, "We tend by a secret law of the soul to move toward our mental image of God . . . Were we able to extract from any man a complete answer to the question, 'What comes to mind when you think about God?' we might predict with certainty the spiritual future of that man."**3**

Put another way, what you think about God will shape your destiny in life.

If you think of God as homophobic, racist, and mad at the world, this distorted vision of reality will shape you into a religious bigot who is—wait for it—*homophobic, racist, and mad at the world*.

If you think of God as a Left-Coast, educated, LGTBQ-affirming progressive, that will shape you into the stereotype of the wealthy bohemian with the "We Will Not Tolerate Intolerance" bumper sticker on the back of your hybrid.

(Don't take that as a slam. I'm writing about half of my neighbors and friends.)

If you think of God as the cosmic version of a life coach, there to "maximize your life," that will shape you into a self-helpy yuppie, even if you dress it up and call it following Jesus.

You see what I'm getting at?

The ISIS terrorist beheading the infidel, the prosperity gospel celebrity preacher getting out of his Hummer after late-night drinks with Kanye West, the Westborough Baptist picketer outside a military funeral screaming "God hates f—s!", the Hindu sacrificing a goat to Shiva, the African witch doctor sacrificing a little boy, the U.S. Army sniper praying to God before he takes the shot, the peace activist risking her neck to stop *another* war because she believes in Jesus' teachings on enemy love, the gay singer who stands up at the Grammys and says thank you to God for his song about a one-night stand, the Catholic nun giving up a "normal life" to live in poverty and work for social change—all of these men and women do what they do because of what they believe about God.

So clearly, what we think about God *matters*.

Who God is has profound implications for *who we are*.

Here's the problem: we usually end up with a God who looks an awful lot like *us*.

As the saying goes, "God created man in his own image. And man, being a gentleman, returned the favor."**4**

There is a human bent in *all* of us to make God in our own image.

My friend Scot McKnight is a New Testament professor in Chicago. For years, he taught a class on Jesus, and he would start every semester with two surveys. The first was a set of questions about the student: what they like, dislike, believe, and so on. The second was the same set of questions, but this time about Jesus. He told me that 90 percent of the time, *the answers were exactly the same*.

That's telling, isn't it?

Here's how you know if you've created God in your own image: *he agrees with you on everything*. He hates all the people you hate. He voted for the person you voted for. If you're a Republican, so is he. If you're a Democrat, she is too. If you're passionate about ____, then God is passionate about ____. If you're open and elastic about sexuality, so is he. And above all, he's tame. You never get mad at him or blown away by him or scared of him. Because he's *controllable*.

And, of course, he's a figment of your imagination.

Often what we believe about God says more about *us* than it does about God. Our theology is like a mirror to the soul. It shows us what's deep inside.

Maybe the truth is that we want a God who is controllable because *we* want to be God. *We* want to be the authority on who God is or isn't and what's right or wrong, but we want the mask of religion or spirituality to cover up the I-wanna-be-God reality.

The most ancient, primal temptation, going all the way back to Adam and Eve in the Garden, is to decide for ourselves what God is like, and whether we should live into his vision of human flourishing or come up with our own. All so we "will be like God, knowing good and evil."[5]

This is why theology is so incredibly important.

The word *theology* comes from two Greek words—*theo*, meaning "God," and *logos*, meaning "word." Simply put, theology is a word about God. It's what comes to mind when we think about God.

It's not like some of us are into theology and others aren't. We *all* have a theology. We *all* have thoughts and opinions and convictions about God. Good, bad, right, wrong, brilliant, dangerous—we all theologize.

But the problem is that much of what we think about God is simply wrong.

I know that's blunt, but I don't really know how else to say it.

Much of what we read in the news or see on TV or pick up on the street about God and the way he works is wrong. Maybe not *all* wrong, but wrong enough to mess up how we live.

In the modern world, we start with the assumption that we know what God is like, and then we judge every religion or church or sermon or book based on our view of God.

A while back, I read an interview in *Rolling Stone* with a celebrity who said he grew up in the church but left it in college because he "couldn't believe in a God who would limit sex to one man and one woman for life."[6]

What was shocking to me wasn't the sex part. This *is* the modern world after all. And the dude was a rock star . . .

What was shocking to me was the bizarre twist of logic.

I couldn't believe in a God who _____?

As if what we think and feel about God is an accurate barometer for what he is actually like.

The Scripture writers come at it the other way around. From Moses to Matthew, they just assume *we have no idea what God is like*. In fact, that a lot of what we think about God is totally off base. If history teaches us anything, it's that the majority are often wrong.

And don't think that if you're religious—or even if you're a Christian—you're off the hook. Jesus spent the bulk of his time helping religious people see that a lot of what they thought about God was wrong too.

You've heard it said . . .

But I say to you . . .

Or he would start a teaching by saying, "The kingdom of God is *like . . .*" and then tell a story that was radically out of step with how people in his day and age thought.

For Jesus and all the writers of Scripture, the starting point for all theology is the realization that:

we don't know what God is like, *but we can learn*.

But to learn, *we have to go to the source*.

And that means we need revelation. Otherwise we end up with all sorts of erroneous and goofy and untrue and maybe even toxic ideas about God.

By "revelation," I don't mean the last book of the Bible or foldout charts from the 1970s about the end of the world. I mean, God himself has to reveal to us what he's like. He has to pull back the curtain of the universe and let you and me look inside. But here's the thing: revelation, by definition, is usually a *surprise*. A twist in the story. A break from the status quo. So when God reveals himself, it's almost always different from what we expect.

All of which leads us to Moses on the top of Mount Sinai.

Yup. That's where we're going.

I am a follower of Jesus, not a Muslim or Hindu or Buddhist or Jedi Knight (sadly). So everything I think about God is through the lens of the Scriptures and then Jesus himself.

Scripture is first and foremost a story. And it's a story about God. We want to make it a story about *us*—about how to get ahead in life or have great sex or up our portfolio or just be happy. And there are all sorts of "success principles" in the Bible, but honestly, that's just not what the story is about. If you strip the Bible down to the core, it's a story about God, and about how we as people relate to God.

And in the story, there are climactic moments when the door swings open and we get a brand-new, compelling, and at times terrifying vision of who God is.

Often these moments take place on a mountain.

If you've ever read the Bible, you know that the second book is called *Exodus*.[7] The setting for the book is Israel in the desert, en route from slavery in Egypt to freedom in a new land. But it's a bumpy ride, to say the least.

At the head of the people of God is the prophet Moses, who has a totally unique relationship with the Creator. We read that God "would speak to Moses face to face, as one speaks to a friend."[8]

In Exodus 33, we get to eavesdrop on a conversation between Moses and God. Moses is asking for God to go with the Israelites every step of the way, and at one point he asks, "Now show me your glory."[9]

In ancient Hebrew literature like *Exodus*, to speak of God's glory was to speak of his *presence* and *beauty*.[10] Moses is asking to see God for who he really is. To see God in person.

For Moses, head knowledge isn't enough. He wants to *experience* God.

God graciously tells Moses that he can't see his face or he will die, "for no one may see me and live."[11] But he'll do him one better. God tells him, "I will cause all my goodness to pass in front of you, and I will proclaim my name, the LORD [Yahweh], in your presence."[12]

So *God*

has a *name*.

The next morning, Moses gets up early and climbs to the top of Mount Sinai. Then we read one of the most staggering paragraphs in the entire Bible.

"The LORD [Yahweh] came down in the cloud and stood there with him and proclaimed his name, the LORD [Yahweh]. And he passed in front of Moses, proclaiming, 'The LORD [Yahweh], the LORD [Yahweh], the compassionate and gracious God, slow to anger, abounding in love and faithfulness, maintaining love to thousands, and forgiving

wickedness, rebellion and sin. Yet he does not leave the guilty unpunished; he punishes the children and their children for the sin of the parents to the third and fourth generation.'"[13]

This is one of those watershed moments when *everything* changes. It's one of the few places in the entire Bible where God describes himself. Where he essentially says, "This is what I'm like." Think of it as God's self-disclosure statement, his press release to the world.[14]

Because of that, it's quite possibly **the most quoted passage *in* the Bible, *by* the Bible.**[15]

The writers of the Bible circle back to this passage over and over and *over* again. *Dozens* of times. Moses and David and Jeremiah and Jonah—they quote it and allude to it and pray it and sing it and claim it and complain about it, but above all, they *believe* it.

This is ground zero for a theology of God.

But what's striking to me is how very different this passage is from what you would expect.

For those of us who live in the West, we tend to think of God in the categories of philosophy. Pick up a book about God, and it'll often start with the omnis . . .

God is omnipotent (he's all-powerful).

God is omniscient (he's all-knowing).

God is omnipresent (he's everywhere at once).

And all of that is true. I believe it.[16] But here's my hang-up: when God describes himself, he doesn't start with how powerful he is or how he knows everything there is to know or how he's been around since before time and space and there's no one else like him in the universe.

That's all true, but apparently, to God, it's not the most important thing.

When God describes himself, he starts with his *name*. Then he talks about what we call *character*. He's compassionate and gracious; he's slow to anger; he's abounding in love and faithfulness, and on down the list.

Which makes sense. Starting with the omnis is kind of like somebody asking about my wife, and me saying she's thirty-three years old, five foot one, 120 pounds, black hair, brown eyes, Latin American ancestry . . .

That's all true, but if you sat there as I was spouting off all these facts about my wife, my guess is that at some point, you would interrupt me and ask, "Yes, but what is she *like*? Tell me about *her*. What's her personality? Is she laid-back or type A? Social or shy? What is she passionate about? What made you fall in love with her? What makes her, *her*?"

Most of the time, this is how we talk about God—we rattle off a bunch of stuff about God that is true; it's just not the stuff that makes him, *him*.

That's why this passage in Exodus is such a breath of fresh air. It turns out that God is better than any of us could imagine.

Now, maybe you've read this passage before in passing, or maybe it doesn't ring a bell, but this passage is *central* to the story of the Bible. The rabbis make a huge deal out of it. In Jewish culture, it's called the "Thirteen Attributes of Mercy," and orthodox Jews pray it on holy days like Yom Kippur, before reading the Torah, and at the synagogue.[17] It's like the John 3v16 of Judaism. If you've spent any time in the church, I'm sure you know John 3v16 like the back of your hand: "For God so loved the world . . ." But oddly enough, little or nothing is said in most churches about Exodus 34v6–7, even though it's quite possibly the most quoted passage *in* the Bible, *by* the Bible.

Let's change that, shall we?

Now, here's the map for how we'll come at this book . . .

We'll talk about Exodus 34v6–7 *line by line*, taking time to soak our imaginations in each word. Each chapter will run something like this:

First, we'll talk about the original Hebrew. It's amazing what you can find when you dig into the language.

In TWO: Stories, we'll look at a story or two where this passage is quoted by later Scripture writers—stories where we see God display his character.

Then in THREE: Jesus, we'll fast-forward to Jesus. As a follower of Jesus, I very much believe that the God on top of Mount Sinai—the God of thunder and lightning and fire and smoke and a voice like a trumpet blast with a subwoofer in the back trunk—took on flesh and blood as the rabbi Jesus of Nazareth. And in Jesus, we see more clearly than ever before what God is like.

And finally, in FOUR: Us, we'll take a step back and think about what *who God is* means for *who we are*, and how it has the potential to reshape our lives from the ground up, unlocking the weights that hold us back from the full, deep, wide, boundless, difficult, invigorating, I-can't-believe-this-is-my-life kind of existence that God made us for and Jesus put on display.

Sound like a plan?

I hope you're sitting there and thinking to yourself, *Let's do this*.

Now, before we wrap up this opening salvo, let me put all my cards on the table.

Writing a book about God is terrifying. Who am *I*? Not only is it a daunting task, but think about what's at stake.

You could read this book and get a *wrong* view of God. That would be no small blunder on my part.

Or you could read this book and radically overhaul the way you relate to God, and in doing so, terraform your life from the ground up.

So as I sit here typing away, I feel both the pulse and throb of my heart beating through my chest—this sense that I *have* to write this. But I also feel this weight on my shoulders. This gravity and seriousness. This sense that I've got to get this right.

So I'll do my very best, but in the end, well, I'm not God.

And even if I *was* God, and this book was the transcript of my conversation with John Mark Comer, you would still walk away with questions, just like Moses did. And the poet Job. And the prophet Habakkuk. And the disciple Peter. And pretty much every single person who has ever had an encounter with the God who is totally Other.

There is a mystery to God that we never quite figure out. After all, we're dealing with a being who is totally unlike any other in the universe.

It's not like you'll finish reading this book, lean back in your chair, and think to yourself, *I got this*.

That's not how it works.

At one point in *Exodus*, Moses asks God his name, and God answers: "I AM WHO I AM."[18]

Well, that *really* clears things up, doesn't it?

God can be mysterious and vague and elusive and hard to catch at times. At the top of Mount Sinai was a cloud, not an engineering schematic. And everybody was invited up the mountain, but only Moses had the courage to step into the cloud.

So I say we start with Moses' prayer: *Show me your glory.*[19]

Even if all we see is a glimpse and all we hear is an echo, it's more than worth the trek.

But before we start the journey, ask yourself, *Do I have the courage to step into the cloud?*

It's one thing to read a book about God; it's another thing to scale a mountain in the middle of the desert and plunge headfirst into the darkness. To abandon yourself to a life of dangerous, risky, I-won't-stop-for-anything pursuit of God.

Hopefully this book will give you the courage to climb the mountain, no matter what you find at the top.

Chapter 1

"**The LORD [Yahweh]**, the LORD [Yahweh], the compassionate and gracious God, slow to anger, abounding in love and faithfulness, maintaining love to thousands, and forgiving wickedness, rebellion and sin. Yet he does not leave the guilty unpunished; he punishes the children and their children for the sin of the parents to the third and fourth generation."

One simple idea that could radically alter how you relate to God: a name

So God has a name.

And just to clarify, it's not *God*.

It's Yahweh.

That might sound unimportant, like it's just semantics. Trust me, it's not. The fact that God has a name is *way* more important than most of us realize. I would argue it has the potential to radically alter the way we relate to God.

I mean, *Yahweh*.

But first, a little backstory . . .

In ancient writings like the Bible, a name was way more than a label you used to make a dinner reservation or sign up for a spin class or file your taxes with the IRS.

Your name was your identity, your destiny, the truth hidden in the marrow of your bones. It was a one-word moniker for the truest thing about you—your inner essence. Your inner Tom-ness or Ruth-ness.

One Old Testament scholar writes, "In the world of the Hebrew Scriptures a personal name was often thought to indicate something essential about the bearer's identity, origin, birth circumstances, or the divine purpose that the bearer was intended to fulfill."[1]

Names are revelatory of the *nature* of a person.

Think of the story of Abraham. Originally, he is just called Abram. But then Yahweh makes him a promise: "I have made you a father of many nations. I will make you very fruitful; I will make nations of you, and kings will come from you."[2]

And then God *renames* him—

from Abram

to Abraham.

Now, look at this.

Abram means "exalted father."

Abraham means "father of many nations."

It's more than a new label. It's a new identity, a new destiny.

And it's not just Abram/ham. Think of his son Isaac. Isaac means "laughter." When his mom, Sarah, heard that she would have a son in her old age, it was so preposterous that she started to laugh. So when Sarah finally gave birth to the miracle child, Abraham named him *Laughter*.

Or think of Isaac's son Jacob. Jacob means "heel grabber," a euphemism for a liar and a cheat. And his biography is exactly that—one con after another. Until an odd story where he wrestles with God and says, "I will not let you go unless you bless me."[3] Then God *renames* him, from Jacob to Israel, which means "he struggles with God." From then on, he's a changed man.

Is this coming into focus for you? Getting clearer? Names were way more than labels to pick up your coffee at the end of the bar. Names were your autobiography in one word.

So when Moses is on Mount Sinai, asking to see God's glory and instead Yahweh says, "I will proclaim my *name*, the LORD [Yahweh], in your presence,"[4] it's an incredibly weighty and significant moment. God is saying that he'll reveal his *identity* to Moses. He'll let Moses in on his inner God-ness, the deepest reality of his being.

And this climactic moment of revelation doesn't come out of nowhere. It's the apex of a long, drawn-out story that's been gathering motion and speed ever since the opening page of the Bible.

TWO: Stories

Let's take a few minutes and trace this story line through the Scriptures . . .

In the first line of *Genesis*, we read, "In the beginning God created the heavens and the earth."

Before there was time and space and Adam and Eve and sex and ice cream and New York City and Instagram, there was a God who *was*.

But so far in the story, this mysterious Creator-of-everything doesn't have a name. Later in *Genesis*, the Creator comes to Abram. He calls him to abandon the worship of his Mesopotamian gods and to go a new land. To pack up the U-Haul and head south on I-5, with no clue where he's going. A gigantic leap of faith.

Abram goes.

And becomes Abraham.

Abraham's relationship with the Creator is stunning. So stunning that three of the major world religions trace their roots back to

Abraham's encounter with God.[5] But even Abraham doesn't ever learn God's name.

When God comes to Abraham, he says, "I am God Almighty."[6]

In the original language, it's, "I am *El Shaddai*."

El was the Canaanite word for the king of the gods.

The Creator calls himself *El Shaddai*, which is a way of saying, "I'm like *El*, but *I'm so much more*."

In other places, God calls himself "*El Elyon*" (God Most High)[7] or "*El Olam*" (God Everlasting),[8] to put it in language that would make sense to Abraham and his world.

Usually, he's just called "the God of Abraham."

Which god?

The god my dad worshiped.

Oh, *that* one.

All that changes when we get to Moses. In one of the best-known stories in the Bible, the Creator calls to Moses out of a bush on fire in the blistering heat of the Sinai Peninsula. Moses was a Hebrew—one of the descendants of Abraham. And by this point in the story, the Hebrews were in a bad spot—in slavery in Egypt, the global military superpower of the day.

So the Creator comes to Moses and says, "I am the God of your father, the God of Abraham, the God of Isaac and the God of Jacob."[9]

Basically, "I'm your dad's god."

Then God and Moses get into a conversation. And yes, you heard me right—a *conversation*. The first of many. God tells Moses that he sees the injustice, the oppression of Israel. He's ready to do something about it. He wants Moses to lead them out of slavery.

To which Moses basically responds, *Wait—what?!*

But after God talks Moses into it (God can be pretty convincing), Moses wants to know what he should tell the Israelites when they ask him about this God. Apparently going back to them and saying *my dad's God wants to set you free* just won't cut it.

And Moses' question is fascinating. In Hebrew, it's *mah shemo?* And it's translated, "What is his name?"[10]

But if you were an ancient Hebrew reader, your ears would perk up right here. It's different from the typical way you would have asked someone their name. If you lived in a Hebrew refugee camp in 1500 BC, you would walk up to a stranger and ask, "*Miy shimka?*" which is more literally, "Who is your name?"[11]

But that's not what Moses asks. He asks, "*Mah shemo?*"

And as we all know, the difference between a *miy shimka?* and a *mah shemo?* is legendary.

Mah shemo? is more like, "What is the meaning of your name?" Or, "What is the significance of your name?" Or, "What makes you . . . you?"

Moses isn't just asking for a label like Bob or Hank or Lazer. (I actually know a kid named Lazer. How cool is that?) He's asking the Creator God, "Who are you? What are you like? Tell me about your character."

And that's when the Creator speaks his name. For the first time. Ever. I imagine a tremor in the ground under Moses' feet . . .

"I AM WHO I AM."

In Hebrew, it's *ehyeh-asher-ehyeh*.

One of the ways to translate this Hebrew phrase is "whatever I am, I will be." Meaning, whatever this God is like, he's that way consistently. He's unshifting, stable, 24/7.

So, for example, if God is compassionate, *then he's compassionate all the time.*

If God is gracious, *then he's gracious all the time.*

If he's slow to anger, *then he's slow to anger all the time.*

Have you ever *thought* you knew somebody really well? Trusted them deeply? Thought they were a stand-up person, and then you get the email, the phone call, the knock at the door, and you discover a shocking double life hidden in the shadows?

Actually, your friend is wanted by the police.

Actually, the story she fed you is a lie.

Actually, your husband is a cheater.

God's not like that. There's no facade. No "once you actually get to know him." He's true to his character. This is a God you can rely on.

So God tells Moses his name and then tells him to go back to Egypt and convey to the Hebrews the following:

"Say to the Israelites, 'The Lord [Yahweh], the God of your fathers—the God of Abraham, the God of Isaac and the God of Jacob—has sent me to you.'

> "This is my name forever,
>> the name you shall call me
>> from generation to generation."**12**

For those of you thinking, *Wait, I'm confused. Why is God called Yahweh here? I thought his name was "I am who I am"* . . .

Okay, stay with me, this next part is a little technical. Okay, it's *really* technical. But strap in tight, because there's a huge payoff if you can survive the next page or two . . .

In ancient Hebrew, there were no vowels in the written language. That sounds crazy, but imagine a world with no computers or even paper and pens. A world where you had to carve every letter into clay or stone. Writing was all about economy. And writing with no vowels actually works pretty well.

Imagine if I wrote, "Ths s sntnc."

Can you see it?

Yeah . . .

Well done.

It says, "This is a sentence."

That's what reading ancient Hebrew is like.

(Some of you are thinking, *I* never *want to read ancient Hebrew. Fair point.*)

Here's why this matters: in God's name—Yahweh—the vowels aren't in the original text. The Hebrew Bible just reads, "*Y-H-W-H*." Four letters, that's all.

In scholarship they call this the *tetragrammaton*, and it was the energy source used by Doc Brown for the flux capacitor.

I'm just kidding about that last part.

Tetragrammaton is a Greek term that means "four-letter word"—but not *that* kind of four-letter word.

YHWH is from the exact same root word as I AM WHO I AM, but *ehyeh* is in the first person, and *Yahweh* is in the third person.[13] Say them out loud right now, and you'll notice the similarity.

So . . .

Ehyeh means "I am."

Yahweh means "he is."

Which is why . . .

When God says his name, it's *ehyeh*.

But when *we* say God's name, it's *Yahweh*.

Make sense?

Now, Yahweh is incredibly hard to translate into English for a couple of reasons. For one, we don't actually know what the vowels are because they were never written down. Almost all Hebrew scholars think Yahweh is right, but honestly, it's still a best guess.

But the main reason is that over time the Hebrews stopped saying the name of God out loud. One of the Ten Commandments is,

"You shall not misuse the name of Yahweh your God."[14] Over the years, they grew so scared of accidentally breaking this command that they just stopped saying his name altogether.

Instead, they would call him other names. A popular one was simply *hashem*, "the name." But the most common title was *adonai*, a Hebrew word meaning "Lord." In the ancient Near East, that's what a servant would call his master, so they used that title for God.

This is also where we get the name Jehovah. Anybody remember that name for God? It was big in the 80s.

Jehovah is the vowels from *adonai* put into the consonants of YHWH.

Like this . . .

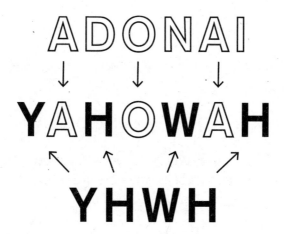

(Note: Hebrew is a guttural language, so the y's sound like j's and the w's sound like v's, hence Jehovah instead of Yahowah. Think Klingon, you Trekkies.)

Okay, we're *almost* through the thick part. Stay with me!

Because of the Jewish switch to *adonai*, usually YHWH is translated into English as "the LORD." This is how the vast majority of translations write out God's name, and so it's what most followers of Jesus call God. We hear it in prayers and songs and teachings and books—it's ubiquitous.

In my opinion, it's a dangerous move that could make us miss out on a key facet of how we relate to God. Why? Because "the LORD" isn't a name; it's a title, like the doctor or the judge or the president. Calling God "the LORD" is like me calling Tammy "the wife." That would be *weird*. Why? Because I'm in a close relationship with her, and that's not the language of intimacy.

What you call somebody says a lot about your relationship.

To my wife I'm *Love*, but to the receptionist at the dentist's office I'm *Mr. Comer*.

To my kids I'm *Dad*, but to the clerk at Whole Foods I'm *sir*.

I'm also son/brother/friend/dude/hey you/pastor/reverend/JM/and—my least favorite of all time—*John-O*! Each of these names says something about the kind of relationship I have with another person.

My sister's name is Elizabeth. She's this gorgeous, tall, mod-elesque blond who lives in Hollywood. Her name is regal, and it's fitting for her person. But I never call her Elizabeth. I call her by her childhood nickname—Betes. No matter how old we get, I'm still the ornery older brother at heart. She *hates* the name Betes. If she ever reads this book, I doubt I'll get a Christmas present for the next five years. But I'm her brother. An unwritten law of the universe says I have the right to call her by any nickname I choose.

Why? Because I'm in relationship with her. So I don't call her Mrs. Mosser; I call her Betes. I call her by *name*.

In the same way, God wants to be called by his name, not a title. Remember that line of poetry?

> "This is my name forever,
>> the name you shall call me
>> from generation to generation."**15**

I would argue that we need to get back to calling God by his name. I think the gradual shift from calling God "Yahweh" to using the title "the Lord" says something about the human condition. For all our talk about a "personal relationship with Jesus," there's a part of us that's scared of intimacy with God. We see the fire and smoke up the mountain, and we shrink back in fear.

Jesus took this even one step further. He taught us to call God "Father"—the most intimate relational name there is. As one poet so eloquently said, God "waits to be wanted."**16** He's aching for a relationship with you.

Now, back to Moses' question: *mah shemo?* What is the meaning of your name?

Does God answer the question? Kind of, but not really. Moses gets the name—Yahweh—but he doesn't get the meaning or the significance of God's name until later in the story.

A few chapters later, Yahweh says to Moses: "I am the LORD [Yahweh]. I appeared to Abraham, to Isaac and to Jacob as God Almighty [*El Shaddai*], but by my name the LORD [Yahweh] I did not make myself fully known to them."[17]

In other words, Yahweh only showed part of himself to Abraham and his sons. This is God's modus operandi in the Scriptures. He doesn't give revelation all at once, but in bits and pieces, giving his people time to absorb and grapple with who God is.[18]

It's not until Moses is on top of Mount Sinai that we get the full, complete answer to his question about the meaning and signifi- cance of God's name.[19] There, in the terrifying cloud that was God's glory, we read that "God proclaimed his *name* . . .

Yahweh

Yahweh

The compassionate and gracious God

Slow to anger

Abounding in love and faithfulness

Showing mercy to thousands and forgiving wickedness, rebellion and sin

Yet he does not leave the guilty unpunished; he punishes the children and their children for the sin of the parents to the third and fourth generation."

(By the way, for those of you thinking, *What is up with the last line about God punishing kids?* we'll get there later. It's *so* good . . .)

This moment of revelation on Mount Sinai where we learn God's name—it's *the* moment in the Hebrew Bible. The rest of what we call the Old Testament is just story after story of this God in action.

THREE: Jesus

The narrative arc of the Bible is anything but straight. It bends and zigzags and makes wrong turns, but eventually the story all leads to a dramatic climax: the coming of Jesus.

In his biography of Jesus, the New Testament writer John makes a profound statement:

"The Word became flesh and made his dwelling among us. We have seen his glory, the glory of the one and only Son, who came from the Father, full of grace and truth."[20]

It's hard to see it in the English translation, but this language is straight out of Exodus 34.

For example, the phrase "made his dwelling among us" is literally "pitched his tabernacle among us." That's a reference to the tabernacle that Israel put up at the base of Mount Sinai.

"Glory"? That's a reference to the cloud at the top of Mount Sinai.

And "grace and truth" is actually an odd reading of the Hebrew phrase translated as "love and faithfulness." (We'll talk about why later.)

Usually people read "grace and truth" and talk about how Jesus was the perfect balance of grace and niceness and love mixed with truth and backbone and the courage to say what needed to be said.

That's totally true.

It's just not remotely the point that John is making.

John is ripping all this language out of *Exodus*—"tabernacle" and "glory" and "love and faithfulness"—as a way of retelling the Sinai story around Jesus. He's making the point that in Jesus, we see the Creator God's glory—his presence and beauty—like never before. In Jesus, Yahweh *becomes a human being*.

Later in John, we get to eavesdrop on Jesus' prayer to the Father:

"I have revealed your *name* to those you gave me . . . I have made your *name* known to them."[21]

Remember, God's name is a stand-in for his character.

Eugene Peterson translates the verse this way: "I have spelled out your character in detail."[22]

I love it.

In Jesus, we get a new, evocative, crystal-clear glimpse of what God is actually like.

The early Christians were quick to pick up on the gravity of Jesus' claims to be the embodiment of God. In order to become a Christian, there was a statement, a slogan, a creed that you had to say out loud before you could be baptized:

Jesus is Lord.

People would *die* over this statement. Literally. Christians were burned alive and thrown into the mouths of wild beasts in the arena. This phrase had a gravitas to it.

Why?

Well, "Lord" is *kyrios* in Greek. For one, that was the title for Caesar, which made the claim that Jesus is Lord tantamount to treason. The Roman Empire already had a *kyrios*.

But more importantly, for Jews, this was the Greek word that was used to translated the Hebrew word *Yahweh*. So in saying that Jesus is Lord, the first Christians—most of whom were Jewish—were saying that Jesus was Yahweh in flesh and blood.

That's a bold claim to make about an itinerant peasant teacher.

But we see this kind of blatant, provocative language all over the writings of the New Testament. The first Christians were *adamant* that Jesus is the bedrock for everything we believe to be true about God.

For years, I thought of Yahweh in the Old Testament as parallel with the Father in the New. Like Jesus is a newcomer in the story. That's wrong, and dangerous. It leads to a twisted caricature, as if the Father is the grumpy old warmonger in the Old Testament, and Jesus is the son who went off to Berkeley and came home with all sorts of radical ideas about grace and love and tolerance and basically said, "Come on, Dad, let's not kill everybody. How about I die for them instead?"

This is a gross misreading of the story the Scriptures tell.

Jesus is the long-awaited human coming of Yahweh, the God on top of Sinai.

FOUR: Us

Whew . . .

You still alive out there? If so, well done. That was a lot to take in. Now, let's take a step back and talk about the staggering implications this has for how we relate to God. Honestly, this was life-changing for me.

For starters, this means that **God is a person**. By person, I don't mean he's male or female or human.[23] By person, I mean he's a relational being. Not an impersonal energy force or a chapter in a systematic theology textbook or a world religion. He's a relational being who wants to, well, *relate*. To people like you and me. He wants to know and be known.

But knowing God isn't just knowing a bunch of facts *about* God. I'm all for theology—heck, it's kind of what I do for a living—but God isn't a doctrine. He isn't a question on a multiple-choice exam that you study to get right so you can "go to heaven when you die."[24] He's a person who wants to be in a relationship with you.

We hear the cliché "a personal relationship with Jesus" a lot in the church. But honestly, I don't think we have any clue just how explosive this idea is.

Remember how Moses and God had conversations?

Later in the story, we read that God would speak to Moses "face to face, as one speaks to a friend."[25]

God has friends?

Yup.

And Moses and God relate to each other like, well, friends.

Then we read a great story in which Moses vents to Yahweh about how Yahweh has been telling him to lead Israel, but Israel is a dysfunctional mess and Moses feels all alone.

So God says, "My Presence will go with you."

Then Moses asks, "Teach me your ways so I may know you and continue to find favor with you."

And God essentially says, "I will."

Then Moses gets even bolder and says, "Show me your glory."

And God says, "You, me—on the mountain tomorrow."[26]

This is *not* how you would expect a conversation between the Creator of the universe and a human being to go. It has a pliability to it. A bend. A give and take.

It sounds like two friends talking. Almost as if Moses and God are on equal footing. Of course, they *aren't* on equal footing, and that's what makes it so striking.

There's another story in *Exodus* where Israel goes off the rails and starts worshiping other gods. This, after Yahweh had just saved them in the Red Sea and gave them food and water in the middle of nowhere—ridiculous, extravagant love. And they spit on it.

As you can imagine, the God who is slow to anger finally gets angry and tells Moses that he's going to destroy Israel and start over with Moses, take it back to square one, reboot the entire franchise. God is clearly upset.

The theologian Gerry Breshears says, "This is God processing his feelings with a human partner."[27]

God processing his feelings?

I love it.

This isn't the energy-in-the-universe or chapter-3-in-the-systematic-theology-textbook God that a lot of us grew up with. This is a person. A person with *feelings*. Yahweh is mad—understandably—and he makes the decision to wipe Israel off the map.

And what happens?

Moses talks him out of it.

He essentially tells Yahweh, "If you do this, then all the other nations will talk trash about you. You made a promise to lead your people through the desert. Your *name* is at stake here."

Then we read, Yahweh "relented and did not bring on the people the disaster he had threatened."[28]

The word *relented* is *naham* in Hebrew. It can be translated as Yahweh "changed his mind," or even "repented."

Yahweh *naham*ed?

He changed his mind?

He repented?

That's what it says.

Now, that doesn't mean God was in sin or doing anything wrong. The word *naham* carries this idea of regret or remorse over a decision. The idea isn't that God was off base, at all; it's that God was moved emotionally; he regretted his decision to judge Israel so harshly, and so he changed his approach.

All of this leads to a vision of a God who *responds*. Who is open to our ideas, dynamic—involved in our lives, but not "in control" in the automated, what's-going-to-happen-is-going-to-happen-with-or-without-me kind of way.

God is more of a friend than a formula.

Most of religion—including a lot of popular "Christian" religion—is about deciphering the formula to get the life we want from God.

Usually the formula looks something like this:

Morality + religious stuff – sin = God's blessing.

So, for example . . .

<u>Bible reading</u> + <u>church</u> − <u>having sex with my girlfriend</u> =
God's blessing.

As if God was an algorithm for a computer software program that
we just have to plug the right numbers into and—*boom!*—out
comes our dream life.

But God doesn't work this way. If you treat God like a formula,
you'll just end up mad and confused. With God, the math rarely
adds up. God is far more interactive and interesting.

But that said, there is a *pattern* we see all over the Bible:

"If you _____, then I will _____."

For example . . .

"If at any time I announce that a nation or kingdom is to be
uprooted, torn down and destroyed, and *if that nation I warned
repents of its evil, then I will relent and not inflict on it the disaster
I had planned.* And if at another time I announce that a nation
or kingdom is to be built up and planted, and *if it does evil in my
sight and does not obey me, then I will reconsider the good I had
intended to do for it."*[29]

You see the pattern? The if/then?

Notice how *interactive* this is. There's a relational back-and-forth
that few of us have actually come to grips with.

We speak, and God speaks.

We act, and God acts.

We pray, and God answers, but not always in the way we want.

We ask God to show mercy, and he *naham*s.

This isn't a formula. It doesn't always play out like this. But it's a way of being in relationship with God.

Yahweh isn't the "unmoved mover" of Aristotle; he's the relational, dynamic God of Abraham, Isaac, and Jacob. The God who *responds*. Who can be *moved*, influenced, who can change his mind at a moment's notice. And this isn't a *lower* view of God; it's a much *higher* view. The theologian Karl Barth called it the "holy mutability of God."[30] He would be less of a God if he couldn't change his intentions when he wants to, or be open to new ideas from intelligent, creative beings he's in relationship with.[31]

This is so simple, so easy to wrap our heads around, but *hardly any of us interact with God this way*. We read a story about Moses getting God to change his mind, and it sounds shocking because it's so far from our own experience. Most people just explain it away: "Well, it doesn't *actually* mean that God changed his mind"—because that's just too much to handle.

Maybe because it feels irreverent. I agree. It *does* feel a little irreverent. There are prayers in the Scriptures—in the books

Moses wrote and especially in *Psalms*—where I cringe, half expecting lightning to strike the person dead. But it doesn't. In fact, God seems to love that kind of raw, uncut prayer, skirting the line between blasphemy and desperate faith. He's not nearly as scared of honesty as we are.

Maybe because our theological system is adamant that *God is sovereign* and *in control* and *everything that happens is the will of God*, as if there's some invisible blueprint behind every event in our life—good or bad—some secret script we live out, and we don't dare ask God to deviate from it.[32]

We'll talk more about this in the next chapter, but I deeply believe this way of thinking about God's involvement in our life is *so* far from what the Scriptures teach. The future is not set in stone. The prayers we pray and the decisions we make in the here and now have a direct, line-of-sight effect on what does—or does not—happen down the line.

Because God *responds*.

But often we read these stories about Moses and David and Jesus and Paul and we think,

That was for them, not for me.

As if the point of the Bible is to tell you how *other* people relate to God.

But Jesus came and lived and died and rose from the grave to make the kind of relationship he and Moses had with Yahweh available to *everybody*.

Right before his death, Jesus prayed to the Father, "I have made your name known to them, and will continue to make your name known *in order that the love you have for me may be in them and that I myself may be in them*."**33**

This is Jesus' agenda for his followers—that you and I will *know* Yahweh like he did. And to join Moses and the characters of the Bible in friendship with God.

Think of how this could rewire how you pray.

A lot of people feel guilty because they don't enjoy prayer. Some people dread it. Others just push through it because they know it's the right thing to do. Most of us avoid it.

That's because most of us don't actually *pray*.

Prayer is what Moses did with God in the tent. What Jesus did with the Father in Gethsemane. It's brutally honest, naked, and vulnerable. It's when your deepest desires and fears and hopes and dreams leak out of your mouth with no inhibition. It's when you talk to God with the edit button in the *off* position and you feel safe and heard and loved. It's the kind of relational exchange you can't get enough of.

And our prayers make a difference. Most of us don't actually believe that prayer changes reality. But it does.

The philosopher Dallas Willard wrote, "God's 'response' to our prayers is not a charade. He does not pretend that he is answering our prayer when he is only doing what he was going to do anyway. Our requests really do make a difference in what God does or does not do. The idea that everything would happen exactly as it does regardless of whether we pray or not is a specter that haunts the minds of many who sincerely profess belief in God. It makes prayer psychologically impossible, replacing it with dead ritual at best. And of course God does not respond to this. You wouldn't either."[34]

Prayer can move the hand of God. Prayer can get God to change his mind—think about the gravity of that.

Prayer is when your life trajectory is going in the wrong direction, so you dialogue with God and he *responds* and your life goes *another* way.

This thing was going to happen, but now it's not.

This other thing was *not* going to happen, but now it *is*.

Because I just had a conversation with God.

As the writer James put it, "The prayer of a righteous person is powerful and effective."[35]

Now, there's a lot of mystery here, plenty of unanswered questions. How exactly does God's will interact with our will? The classic "sovereignty versus free will" debate. Honestly? I don't know.

But I'm sure of this: prayer is not just going through the motions. It does something. Our prayers have the potential to alter the course of history. And God's action *in* history is, in some strange way, contingent on our prayers.

My friend Skye Jethani quotes the philosopher Blaise Pascal's line, "God has instituted prayer so as to confer upon His creatures the dignity of being causes" and interprets it like this:

"We are not merely passive set pieces in a prearranged cosmic drama, but we are active participants with God in the writing, directing, design, and action that unfolds. Prayer, therefore, is much more than asking God for this or that outcome. It is drawing into communion with him and there taking up our privileged role as his people. In prayer, we are invited to join him in directing the course of his world."[36]

Oh man, that's so good.

"In prayer, we are invited to join him in directing the course of his world."

From the beginning of human history, God, the Creator of *everything*, has been looking for friends, for free, intelligent, creative partners to collaborate with on running the world.

That's prayer.

If this take on prayer makes you nervous, if it's too close to the edge, if right now you're thinking, *Who am I to come to God that way?* then remember that when you come to God, you come in Jesus' name.

I assume you're familiar with that cliché—"in Jesus' name"? For the record, that was never supposed to be a tag line we drop at the end of a prayer to get what we want. To pray in Jesus' name means two things.

First, it means to pray in line with his character, to pray for the kind of stuff he wants to see happen in the world.

Pray for a new Range Rover or dream vacation to Hawaii, and you may get it, but the odds are God will let you down.

Pray for healing, justice, the courage to stand up for your faith in the corrosive soil of Western secularism, the kind of stuff Jesus is all about? Well, keep your eyes open.

But secondly, and more importantly, to pray in Jesus' name means that whenever we pray, we have the same access to God that Jesus does.

One New Testament scholar said it this way: "To pray in Jesus' name . . . means that we enter into Jesus' status in God's favor, and invoke Jesus' standing with God."[37]

So for those of you thinking, *I can't interact with God in this kind of a back-and-forth way, like a friend or a coworker helping God build out his world. I'm no Moses, and I'm definitely not Jesus!*—true, that makes two of us. But if you're a follower of Jesus, then when you come before God, you come *in Jesus' name*. You invoke his status with God. You come, not as a beggar off the street, but as a royal daughter or son of the Father.

And what you find waiting for you is Yahweh, the *person*, who wants to *relate* to you.

And you don't even have to climb a mountain. All you have to do is open your lips.

Chapter 2

Chapter 2

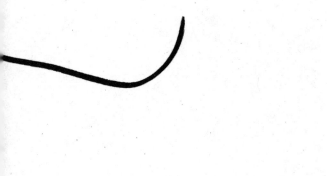

"The LORD [Yahweh], **the LORD [Yahweh]**, the compassionate and gracious God, slow to anger, abounding in love and faithfulness, maintaining love to thousands, and forgiving wickedness, rebellion and sin. Yet he does not leave the guilty unpunished; he punishes the children and their children for the sin of the parents to the third and fourth generation."

Why does God need a name in the first place? GOD and the "gods"

Ever been to India?

If not, you really should go; it's stunning.

I went a few years back, and now I see the world differently. It's like my eyes were opened to what's been there all along.

India is a place with no parallel. It's beautiful, in every way. The people, the culture, the landscape—it's colorful and multisensory and vibrant and exotic and strange, and there are so. many. people.

But to me, the most fascinating thing is the spiritually charged atmosphere.

There are literally millions of gods in the Hindu pantheon, so everywhere you look, there are temples and shrines and idols and priests in ochre-colored robes praying and incense burning and animals dying in sacrifice to Shiva or Vishnu or one of the "gods."[1]

I was there visiting an orphanage started by a couple in our church. They call it "Happy Home for the Handicapped." In the Hindu caste system, if a child is born with a disability or deformity, they believe you are Dalit, one of the untouchables. It's your karma, or punishment for sins in a past life.[2] In some circles, the Dalit are thought of as subhuman, there to suffer for their past mistakes and do all the jobs nobody else wants—no hope but to die and be reborn into a higher caste and a better life. Some parents will literally drop off their disabled newborn on the side of the road and drive away.[3]

Happy Home is a place just for kids like that—who have been abandoned, thrown out, left to die.

To be honest, I was scared to see it in person. That much pain and suffering in one room made me nervous. I was expecting it to be a sad, lonely, disturbing place—children missing limbs, boys who couldn't walk, girls who couldn't see. All living in poverty with no parents or family. But here's the shocking reality: the thing that stands out most about Happy Home is that, well, it's *happy*. And by happy, I mean throbbing with joy. Everywhere you look, you see bright, white teeth cracking open dark skin, smiles as wide as the horizon, unstoppable laughter—and it far outshines all the pain and ache and this-isn't-how-it-should-be-ness of an orphanage.[4]

Walking into Happy Home is like walking into a birthday party that never ends. A celebration. I'm pretty sure it's the kind of thing Jesus had in mind when he said, "The kingdom of God has come near."[5]

But then you walk back outside and you see people sacrificing chickens to Shiva on the street corner and goat blood churning in the roadside ditch as a priest chants a prayer to his divinity of choice.

And you *feel* it—the energy, the electricity in the air, the spirituality.

But the crazy thing—at least for a Westerner like me—is that it doesn't feel fake, like a hoax or a sham or a primitive superstition that one day "these non-Westerners will get over."

It feels *real*.

When you walk past an idol or a temple, it feels like . . . *something is there*.

Have you ever had that kind of an experience? At a temple or in a yoga studio or by the park down the street from your house, where something spiritual was going down and your Western, secular brain tries to explain it away as nonsense but you just can't get rid of this nagging sense that there's something to it?

What *is* that?

That's what this chapter is about.

Now, to recap: the plan for this book is to work through Exodus 34v6–7 *line by line*, because it's quite possibly the most quoted passage *in* the Bible, *by* the Bible.

The last chapter was about how God is Yahweh.

This chapter is about how God is—*wait for it*—Yahweh.

Think back to the opening line: *Yahweh, Yahweh, the compassion-ate and gracious God . . ."*

Notice that Yahweh repeats his name.

Why?

In the modern world, if you're writing a book or a blog post or an email and you want to emphasize a point, you *italicize* it or <u>under-line</u> it or **bold** it or PUT IT IN ALL CAPS. But in the ancient world, if you wanted to really drive a point home, you would repeat it.

I mean, if you really wanted to make a point that everybody would catch, you would say it *again*.

See what I just did right there?

When Yahweh says his name, not once, but *twice*, it's his way of saying that he wants us to slow down and think about his name in depth.[6]

So let's do that . . .

In the last chapter we learned:

God's name isn't *God*.

God's name is *Yahweh*.

But this raises a provocative, disturbing question: Why does God need a name in the first place?

What's wrong with *God*?

In fact, why is God rarely called "God" in the Scriptures?[7] Why is he usually called "Yahweh" or "Yahweh God"?

Short answer—and hang on, this might hit you like a freight train: because there are *many* "gods."

Now, we have a lot of ground to cover, so buckle up. Here we go . . .

TWO: Stories

As long as I'm repeating myself, think back to the opening line of the Bible: "In the beginning God created the heavens and the earth." In Hebrew, the word *God* is *elohim*. As I said before, it's not a name; it's a category. It's used for the Creator of the universe, but here's the thing: it's also used for all sorts of *other* spiritual beings.

An *elohim* is an invisible-but-real spiritual creature.[8]

And right off the bat—in the opening line of the story—we know there is one *elohim* who made *everything*. The sun, the moon, the stars, the freckles you get on your nose in late July—he made *all* of it.

This was a staggering claim to make in 2000 BC.[9] However you read Genesis 1, this much is clear: the story is set against the backdrop of a number of *other* ancient creation myths, like the Babylonian *Enuma Elish*. Each one is a little different, but they all basically claim that the universe was created in the aftermath of a giant, cosmic conflict between the "gods."

In the *Enuma Elish*, the "god" Marduk leads an epic battle against Tiamat and her monster army. He kills her and then makes planet Earth out of her corpse.

This explains why you occasionally get dizzy.

As crazy as it sounds to modern ears, this was how intelligent, thinking people made sense of the world.

But the Bible claims something radically out of step with its time. It claims there is *one true Creator God* who made *everything*. And the world was born, not out of conflict or war or jealous infighting, but out of the overflow of his creativity and love.

So there's God—the uncreated Creator of everything. A being with no parallel in the universe.

And then there's the "gods"—created, invisible-but-real spiritual beings.

Whoever these other *elohim* are, they aren't even in the same category. But that doesn't mean these other "gods" are a sham . . .

In the second book of the Bible, *Exodus*, we read about Yahweh saving Israel out of slavery in Egypt. There's a line in Exodus 12 where Yahweh says, "I will bring judgment on all the gods of Egypt."[10]

Most of you know the story of the ten plagues, but what you may not know is that many of the plagues are directed at a specific Egyptian deity.[11]

For example, Amun-Ra was the sun god in the Egyptian pantheon. He was also the king over all the other Egyptian deities of choice.

So what does Yahweh do?

He blots out the sun.

For three days, it's pitch-black. This is Yahweh's version of stick-it-to-the-man. It's his way of saying, "Amun-Ra isn't the king over the gods; *I am*."[12]

So Yahweh's relationship with these other pretender "gods" is hostile. It's not an exaggeration to say he's at war with them. In fact, this warfare language is used all over the Hebrew Scriptures.

When Israel is finally out from under Egypt's whip, we read that Yahweh "had brought judgment on their gods."[13]

As one firsthand observer put it, "Now I know that the Lord [Yahweh] is greater than all other gods, for he did this to those who had treated Israel arrogantly."[14]

Notice: all *other* gods.

And what is Israel's response to Yahweh saving them from Egypt and its pantheon? Worship.

We immediately read a song of praise:

> "Who among the gods
>   is like you, Lord [Yahweh]?
> Who is like you—
>   majestic in holiness,
> awesome in glory,
>   working wonders?"[15]

So, because Yahweh is in a class all by himself, and because he saved Israel out of slavery, he is the one and only *elohim* deserving of worship.

Think of all the language in *Psalms*—the worship songs of ancient Israel.[16] Listen to this from Psalm 86:

Among the gods, there is none like you, Lord [Yahweh];
    no deeds can compare with yours.

Or this from Psalm 96:

Great is the Lord [Yahweh] and most worthy of praise;
    he is to be feared *above all gods*.

Or this one is crazy—Psalm 97:

Worship him, *all you gods* . . .
For you, Lord [Yahweh], are the Most High over all the earth;
    you are exalted *far above all gods*.

So even the "gods" are to worship Yahweh. Why? Because he's the "Most High." This language of Yahweh as the Most High means that in the hierarchy of the "gods," Yahweh is at the top—in his own category.

Is your head reeling? I'm just getting started.

Think of the Ten Commandments. What's the very first one?

"You shall have no other gods before me."[17]

Most people skip over this commandment because they *assume* there are no other gods. Right? They're all made-up, a figment of Israel's imagination. And that could be true.[18] But pay close attention: *it doesn't say that*. In fact, it seems to assume there *are* other gods and we're not to worship them. Ever.

Then the second commandment is: "You shall not make for yourself an image [or idol] . . . You shall not bow down to them or worship them; for I, the Lord [Yahweh] your God, am a jealous God."

So, there's a command about "gods."

Then there's a command about idols.

And Israel is to stay away from *both* of them.

Now, most people collapse the first two commandments into one and lump together "gods" and idols. I get it: idols and "gods" are linked together in a symbiotic relationship, but they are *not* the same thing.

We already covered what a "god" is—an invisible-but-real spiritual creature.

An idol, in contrast, is a dead statue, nothing more. A wood or stone or metal carving. It's inanimate. Hand-carved by a crafts-man in need of a buck or a priest in need of a job. It's a totem, a representation of something *else*.

By itself, an idol can't do anything to you—it's a hunk of rock; but the *elohim* that at times are *lurking behind* or *represented by* the idol, imbuing it with power, well, they can. Some of them are actually quite powerful. That's when an idol becomes dangerous, when it becomes a gateway to a real, spiritual being.

Think back to the story of Moses in Pharaoh's throne room. To show that he's really from Yahweh, Moses does miracles.[19]

First he turns his staff into a snake.

But then what happens? Pharaoh's magicians do *the exact same thing*.

I seriously cannot *wait* until this comes out on Netflix . . .

So next Moses turns the Nile River into blood; but Pharaoh's magicians do the same.

Then Moses makes frogs come up out of the Nile and cover the whole of Egypt, but Pharaoh's magicians call on the dark arts and copy his miracle.

You ever read this story and think, *How are they doing this? Magic? Sleight of hand?* Neither. They are priests, linked up with Egypt's "gods." Tuned into the power of these malevolent spiritual creatures.

Finally Moses turns dust into gnats, and the magicians are at a loss.

Apparently gnats are a problem . . .

My point is that these other *elohim* have a certain amount of power even to work miracles. But over and over again, Yahweh warns his people: don't *ever* worship them.

In Deuteronomy 6, we read the great Shema—the most legendary prayer in the Hebrew tradition: "Hear, O Israel: The LORD [Yahweh] our God, the LORD [Yahweh] is one. Love the LORD [Yahweh] your God with all your heart and with all your soul and with all your strength."[20]

There are layers of meaning to this text, but it seems like the primary meaning is that Yahweh is the one true Creator God, over all the others, and you are to love him and him only.

But if you know the tragic story of Israel, this warning falls on deaf ears. Over and over, Israel goes over to the "gods" of the nations.

And if you're still thinking, *Yeah, but these other gods aren't real, right?* stay with me for a few more examples . . .

In the book of *1 Kings*, we read about Israel's zenith under King Solomon. Everything is going incredibly well until the beginning of chapter 11.

"King Solomon, however, loved many foreign women besides Pharaoh's daughter—Moabites, Ammonites, Edomites, Sidonians and Hittites. They were from nations about which the LORD [Yahweh] had told the Israelites, 'You must not intermarry with them [notice why!], because they will surely turn your hearts after their gods' . . . As Solomon grew old, his wives *turned his heart after other gods*, and his heart was not fully devoted to the LORD [Yahweh] his God."[21]

So watch what happens . . .

"He followed Ashtoreth the goddess of the Sidonians, and Molek the detestable god of the Ammonites . . . Solomon built a high place for Chemosh the detestable god of Moab, and for Molek the detestable god of the Ammonites. He did the same for all his foreign wives, who burned incense and offered sacrifices to their gods."[22]

Notice, the writer lists off a number of ancient "gods," but nowhere does the text say these were "false gods"—as in, not real or fake or a con for a superstitious age. Instead, the text calls the "gods" by name.

Ashtoreth is the goddess of Sidon (Lebanon on a current map).

Molek is the god of Ammon (same place as modern-day Amman, Jordan).

Chemosh was over Moab (in another part of Jordan).

These are "gods" with power and authority over *geographic regions* and *ethnic groups*, or what we call nations.

We see this idea of spiritual powers over nations all throughout the Hebrew Bible. In *Daniel*, there's a crazy story about Daniel's prayers going unanswered for three weeks. Finally an angel comes to him from Yahweh and says he was late because "the prince of the Persian kingdom resisted me twenty-one days."[23] The "prince" here is some kind of spiritual being at the back of the Persian Empire. Then as he's leaving, the angel says there's a "prince of Greece" he has to fight as well.[24]

So there's a prince of Persia?

And another one for Greece?

There are "gods" or demons or whatever you want to call these spiritual beings over *people* and *places*? Over entire nations?

Now, don't misread me here. I'm *not* implying that America is a "Christian nation" and that India or Jordan *isn't*.

All I'm saying is that there seem to be spiritual beings with a measure of power and authority over geographic areas and people groups.

Let me flesh out what I mean . . .

As a parent, I'm terrified by the recent uptake in school shootings. I have three kids in our local elementary school, and the thought of that kind of mayhem and carnage coming to my neighborhood sends chills down my spine. But it hit me recently that two of the worst mass shootings in American history were within miles of each other in Colorado: first, at Columbine High School in 1999, where two students gunned down thirteen people, and then in the Aurora massacre in 2012, where a gunman's barrage of bullets inside a movie theater playing *The Dark Knight Rises* left twelve people dead and fifty-nine injured. To top it all off, *four other shootings* have taken place in the same region from Colorado Springs to Denver.[25]

Coincidence?

Probably.

Maybe it's just violent video games and lax gun control laws or something weird about Colorado.

But *maybe*—and this is full-on speculation—there is a spiritual being in that area, and he's malevolent and violent and cruel, with an odd sway and influence over certain desperate people, and every few years we see his handiwork on the news.

Probably not.

I doubt it.

But could it be?

Even if that's a bogus theory, I do know there are areas in my own city where there's a dark, oppressive shadow—something's *there*. You feel it when you walk past a house or through a park or into a store. You have this sense that *you're not alone*, and whatever it is that's here with you isn't good.

One of the most disturbing passages in the entire Bible for me is Psalm 82:

> God presides in the great assembly;
>> he renders judgments among the "gods."

This is one of several places in the Bible where we read about a collection of divine beings over the earth.[26] The NIV translates the

Hebrew as "the great assembly," but a few other translations have "the divine council."[27] The divine council is well-known imagery from the ancient world.[28] It is a way of envisioning heaven as an ancient Near Eastern throne room. Yahweh, the king, is there, with all these other spiritual beings around him.

One Hebrew scholar says it like this: "The heavenly realm appears to be depicted as operating along lines similar to an ancient Near Eastern royal court with the monarch surrounded by counsellors and envoys that advise the king and perform his will."[29]

You see the pagan version of the divine council in that terrible genre of film that mixes Greek mythology with man-rock music and cheesy special effects. I saw one recently where Liam Neeson played Zeus, the king of the gods, in the divine council, looking down on earth from the heavens. I normally like Mr. Neeson, but everybody has low points in their career . . .

And if you're thinking, *Wait, that's in the Bible?*

Kind of.

The difference between ancient *mythology* (see Liam Neeson as Zeus) and Hebrew *theology* is that in the Bible, Yahweh "renders judgment"—he's *over* all the other so-called "gods."

The language in the poem is fascinating:

"God . . . among the 'gods.'"

Or in Hebrew:

"*Elohim* . . . among the *elohim*."

Then the next stanza peels back the curtain to the inner workings of the universe. Keep in mind, this is Yahweh, speaking to the "gods" . . .

> "How long will you defend the unjust
>   and show partiality to the wicked?
> Defend the weak and the fatherless;
>   uphold the cause of the poor and the oppressed.
> Rescue the weak and the needy;
>   deliver them from the hand of the wicked."[30]

Notice what the "gods" are doing: injustice![31] They are wreaking havoc all over the earth. Driving the poor and the weak and the young and the vulnerable into the grave. And Yahweh is saying, "Stop it! Enough is enough. No more violence and murder and genocide and rape and abuse and 'natural' disasters and famine and drought and disease and death."

Knock it off!

The psalm ends like this:

> "I said, 'You are "gods";
>   you are all sons of the Most High.'
> But you will die like mere mortals;
>   you will fall like every other ruler."[32]

Or in today's language, *you're going down.*

And the closing line is a prayer:

> Rise up, O God, judge the earth,
> > for all the nations are your inheritance.

Wow, that's a lot to take in.

Let's take a step back and put together all the pieces: the Scripture writers are all making the same basic point . . .

There is one true Creator God who made the universe and everything in it. He has no equal, and no parallel.

But there is also a multiplicity of other wannabe "gods," invisible-but-real spiritual beings. One scholar I love calls them "gods with a lowercase *g*."[33]

In *The Message*, Eugene Peterson translates Yahweh into English as "God" in all caps.

So there's God.

And then there's the "gods."

Now, I'm not saying that Greek mythology is true and Homer's *Odyssey* is historically accurate. Certainly many of the "gods" we read about were just projections of ancient imaginations. And certainly many of the ancient ideas about the "gods" were totally off base.

But that doesn't mean they are all make-believe.

If this language of the "gods" makes you uncomfortable, I apologize. Kind of. It *is* scriptural, even if it makes you nervous. But I get it: even the later Scripture writers are uneasy with it. By the time we get to Isaiah—one of the last writings before the time of Jesus—we read almost contradictory statements like, "I am the LORD [Yahweh], and there is no other; *apart from me there is no God*."[34] Now, in context this is hyperbole, and poetry at that—not an academic essay on the difference between Yahweh and all the other spiritual beings. The prophet's point is that the gap between Yahweh and the other "gods" is so chasmic, so uncrossable, that these other beings aren't really even worthy of the title "gods."[35]

This is a great example of where we need to give the library that is Scripture a little breathing room to allow for diversity and tension and counterpoints from its various writers.

In the New Testament, you have Paul in his letter to the Corinthians fumbling around for the right language: "For even if there are so-called gods, whether in heaven or on earth (*as indeed there are many 'gods' and many 'lords'*), yet for us there is but one God, the Father, from whom all things came and for whom we live."[36]

You see the tension? The paradox? The difficulty of language? We're not the first ones to get hung up on this.

So if you don't like calling these spiritual creatures "gods," that's fine. I'm sure Isaiah would pat you on the back, and I doubt Paul would chastise you.

Most people in the modern world just call them angels or demons. And that's fine, but there are a few reasons I shy away from that language. For one, it's barely used at all in the Old Testament. The word *demon* is used a whopping two times.[37] Plus, these two words—*angels* and *demons*—come with a truckload of cultural baggage.

We think of angels as blond Swedish supermodels with a ten-foot wingspan.

To clarify, in the Scriptures, every angel we ever read about is male; they don't have wings;[38] and they are *terrifying*—take that, Christmas decor!

And we think of demons as little cartoon characters with horns and a pitchfork larking about on Bugs Bunny's shoulder.

Neither of these lazy caricatures does justice to their reality.

The fact is, there are all sorts of words used in the Scriptures to speak to the spiritually charged universe we inhabit:

- gods
- heavenly beings
- sons of God
- sons of the Most High

- cherubim
- seraphim
- angels
- demons
- princes
- lords
- powers
- principalities
- rulers
- authorities
- spiritual forces of evil
- powers of this dark world
- evil spirits

If you don't like "gods," fine; just swap it out for something else you're more comfortable with. That's great. The point I'm trying to nail down is this: They are *real*. Not fake. Not nonentities. Not a myth from a superstitious age.

But there is *so* much we don't know about these spiritual beings . . .

Where did they come from?

How did they get here?

Why doesn't Yahweh end them *now*?

How long do they live? Forever? Or do they die off?

Do they reproduce?

Are there varying levels of power and authority? It seems like the "gods"/*elohim* are powerful beings with authority over nations, and the demons are more like lower-level beings who do the "gods'" bidding, but we're well into the realm of speculation at that point.

How much power and authority do they actually have?

What about "the Satan"? Is he a person or more of an office? One being or many? How much control does he have over the other *elohim*?

Honestly?

We don't know.

I mean, there is a lot we *do* know. But so much is unclear. It's kind of like the beginning of *Star Wars*. (Isn't everything?) Imagine you're seeing this in 1977, for the very first time . . .

A NEW HOPE

*It is a period of civil war.
Rebel spaceships, striking
from a hidden base, have won
their first victory against
the evil Galactic Empire.*

You get to the end of the crawl, and you're left with all sorts of questions: Why is there a civil war? Who are the rebels? Why is the Galactic Empire bad? Some of those questions get answered in the story; others don't. The point is, you, the reader, are just dropped into the middle of an ongoing story and left to catch up.[39]

The beginning of the Bible is very similar. Think of Genesis 3. There's a *snake* in the Garden. In the ancient Near East, the snake was a well-known symbol for chaos and evil. How did the snake get into Eden? It's unclear.

What *is* clear is that we live in a spiritually dense world, jammed with both human and nonhuman beings beyond measure.

It's also clear that these spiritual beings, just like humans, have a measure of free will and autonomy. They can obey and serve Yahweh, or they can rebel and war against him, just like us.

Some of them love the Creator God; others hate and rage against his existence.

Some of them are good; others are evil and noxious and sadistic and cruel.

And all throughout the story of God, the dominant sins of Israel are idolatry and her good friend injustice. Idolatry and injustice populate page after page of the Hebrew Scriptures. But the temptation was never to worship Yahweh *or* _____. It was always, Yahweh *and* _____. For Israel to live in a polyamorous relationship with the "gods" rather than stay faithful to her true husband. And the by-product of this illicit affair is injustice—it tears apart the social fabric of the world.

But over and over again, Israel goes over to these other "gods," because they give them what they want. The "gods" are like the politician who will do or say *anything* to get in power, so he makes all sorts of promises and claims it will cost the people nothing. But when he's finally in power, his true nature comes out, and it's not good.

At some point, the Old Testament starts to feel like the same story on repeat. You get this nagging sense of déjà vu. Israel goes after the other "gods"; it goes badly; they ask for mercy; and Yahweh comes to save them.

This happens about a bajillion times.

Which is why Psalm 82 is a prayer for God *to do something about it*. To end the tyranny of these evil, wicked powers. To drive them out. Put a stop to their havoc. And set the world free.

This, of course, is where Jesus comes in . . .

THREE: Jesus

As I said before, Jesus comes as the embodiment of Yahweh himself, the in-flesh-and-blood-ing of the Creator God.

As the New Testament writers look back on Jesus' life, death, and resurrection, they make it clear that one of Jesus' primary agendas was to disarm the powers at war with Yahweh.

Listen to the writer John's summary of Jesus' work: "The reason the Son of God came was *to destroy the works of the devil.*"[40]

Or here's a biopic from the writer Luke: "God anointed Jesus of Nazareth with the Holy Spirit and power, and . . . he went around doing good and *healing all who were under the power of the devil.*"[41]

Mark gets right to the point: "He traveled throughout Galilee, preaching in their synagogues *and driving out demons.*"[42]

In the Old Testament, we don't read *one* story about an exorcism. Zero. But the Gospels are chock-full of stories about Jesus casting out all sorts of demons. What exactly is going on here?

Simple: Yahweh is answering Psalm 82's prayer. He's coming to put an end to the "gods'" injustice.

Nowhere is this more clear and compelling than in Jesus' death and resurrection. For a brief moment, it looks like Yahweh has lost the war. His Son is hanging limp on a cross, all the life gone out of his body. It feels like the end. But three days later, the tomb is empty, and Jesus is *alive*. His resurrection breaks the spine of death itself, not through violence, but through sacrificial love.

Paul says it this way in *Colossians*: "Having disarmed the powers and authorities, he made a public spectacle of them, triumphing over them by the cross."[43]

He made a public spectacle of them.

He put them to shame.

He did a victory dance in the end zone.

This is the most basic, most ancient reading of the cross.

Ever since the Protestant Reformation, the primary metaphor by which we understand the cross is called "substitutionary atonement." It's the idea that Jesus died in our place to make us right with God.

It's true. I believe it.

But it's one of several metaphors in the New Testament for all that happened through Jesus' death and resurrection. And it may come as a surprise to learn that for more than a millennium and a half, the dominant metaphor wasn't substitutionary atonement; it was another one, called *Christus Victor*. For those of us who don't speak Latin, that means "Christ is victorious." The idea behind *Christus Victor* is simple: Yahweh has been at war with the spiritual powers of the universe for millennia. And the cross is the decisive blow in his campaign against evil. The breakthrough victory. On the cross, Jesus defeated Satan, his pantheon of wild and dangerous beings, and even death itself.[44]

Is this what comes to mind when you think of the cross?

Hopefully yes, but for a lot of people, the honest answer is no. But this has a direct effect on how we follow Jesus.

Think of it like this: what D-Day was to World War II, Jesus' death and resurrection were in the war against the evil powers. For those of you who are a little fuzzy on your American history, D-Day was the day the Allies retook the beaches of France. By the next morning, June 7, 1944, Hitler and his Nazi regime were done. They had no chance of winning. But it was followed by a full *year* of bloody, ghastly fighting from the beaches of Normandy to the center of Berlin.

We live between D-Day and VE-Day. Between Jesus' first coming to land the decisive blow and his second to end evil for good. And in the meantime, our job is to stand in that victory. To hold our ground. To cooperate with heaven's invasion of earth.

Yes, we "fight," but our fight isn't with swords or spears or AK-47s; it's with prayer and sacrificial love. So don't join a militia and go to war; get on your knees and give your life away.

Because there is an invisible world *all around us* that is just as real as the one we can see and touch and taste and smell.

A few thoughts on worldview . . .

This really comes down to worldview. Your worldview is how you *see* the world. Think of it like a pair of glasses you put on every morning before you go about your day.

Most Westerners don't buy the idea of an invisible world all around us. It feels like superstitious nonsense from premodern man. I mean, come on. We're educated. We know better. We have Wikipedia.

Even as followers of Jesus, it's easy to get sucked into the secular framework. Yes we believe in angels, but we don't really think about them, other than on Christmas Eve. And demons? Sure, I guess. But we act like all the demonic beings went into retirement around 70 AD and moved to Indonesia.

Because this is the worldview we grew up immersed in.

But is it the worldview of Jesus and the Scripture writers?

As I see it, there are three major worldviews, all vying for king of the hill.

First is **polytheism**. *Poly* means "many," and *theism*, "gods." It's the idea that there are *many gods*. Gods of the mountain, gods of the valley, gods of the sea, gods of the farm and field. And here's the key: gods of equal or parallel power and authority.

As a worshiper, you pick one based on where you live or what you fear or want.

Then you make sacrifices to get the god(s) on your good side.

They aren't monogamous, so worship one or worship fifty—it doesn't matter. But whatever you do, *don't* make them angry.

Polytheism

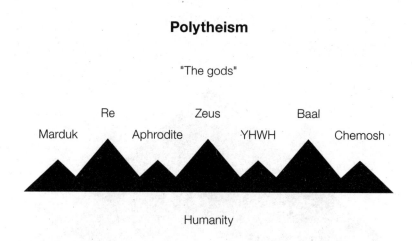

"The gods"

Re   Zeus   Baal

Marduk   Aphrodite   YHWH   Chemosh

Humanity

Clearly, this is *not* the worldview of Jesus.

On the other side of the ring is a relative newcomer on the scene: **universalism**. This worldview is all over my city. I would say it's the dominant view of our time. Basically the idea is that out there, somewhere in the universe, there is one God, not many. Maybe this "God" is a he/she/they/it/me/state-of-being— who are *we* to say? And when it comes to the multiplicity of world religions, the idea is that "all paths lead up the same mountain." So whether you're a Christian or a Jew or a Muslim or a Hindu or a Wiccan priest, it doesn't really matter. In the end, it all gets you to God.

Universalism

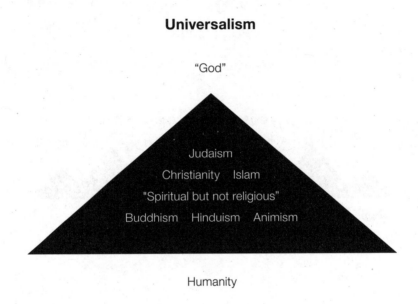

"God"

Judaism
Christianity   Islam
"Spiritual but not religious"
Buddhism   Hinduism   Animism

Humanity

Sadly, this is not the worldview of Jesus either.

At times I wish it was. It sounds so nice and open-minded and hip.

Actually, if you know its origins, it's nothing of the kind. This view comes out of European imperialism.[45] Around the turn of the nineteenth century, as the British and their European friends were out colonizing the world, they were exposed to all sorts of new forms of spirituality. Animism in Africa. Islam in the Middle East.

Ancestor worship in Southeast Asia. Hinduism in India. Buddhism in Japan.

Most of the men out colonizing the "uncivilized" world were deists, meaning they believed in some kind of a God, but thought he made the world and then walked away, conveniently leaving it for them to conquer.

And as these men learned about the diversity of faith all over the world, they started to notice common themes in the teachings of Jesus and Muhammad and Buddha and all the major world religions. And so they thought, *You know, all these religions are basically saying the same thing. They must all come around to the same place in the end*.

And there are similarities among the world religions, between, say, the teachings of Jesus and the Buddha. For sure.

But there are also chasmic, mile-wide, *irreconcilable* differences.

The problem with universalism is that none of the *conquered* people think they are worshiping the same God as everybody else. That's the view of the *conqueror*.

The reality is that all around the world there are very different people worshiping very different "gods."

All of which leads me to the last and final worldview, which I believe is that of Jesus and the writers of the Bible. It's called **monotheism**.

Now, the basic idea behind monotheism is easy: *mono* means "one." There is *one* God. But this isn't a word used by Jesus or any of the writers of the Bible, so we have to be careful in how we define it.

Here's how a lot of Western Christians understand monotheism:

One way to think about monotheism

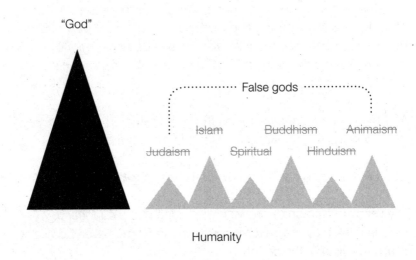

There's no place for any other "gods" in the paradigm. They assume they aren't even real. And the one and only way to "get up the mountain" is through Jesus.

But here's a better way to think about it, one that's more in line with the Scriptures:

A better way to think about monotheism

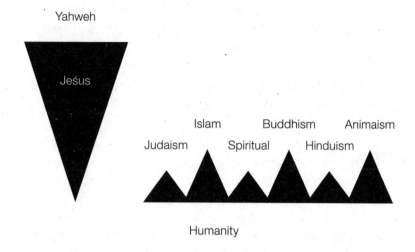

Imagine this: instead of one mountain, *there are many.* And on top of each mountain is a real spiritual being—Zeus or Shiva or the Wiccan mother goddess. Call them "gods" or demons or whatever you feel comfortable with. I like Paul's language of "rulers and authorities in the heavenly realms"[46]—he doesn't clarify if they are good, evil, neutral; he just says they *are.*

And it's not that "all paths lead up the same mountain." It's that there are *different paths* up *different mountains*.

But at the top of the mountain is the *one* true Creator God—over all the others. He's not just bigger and better; he's in a totally other category. And there's no path up his mountain. This God, the only being really worthy of the title "God" in the first place, the one called Yahweh in the Old Testament and "God our Father and the Lord Jesus Christ" in the New[47]—is in heaven, not on earth. And in Jesus, he comes down the mountain. He becomes the rabbi from Galilee to rescue and save the world.

It's not so much that "Jesus is the only way to God." I mean, he *is*, but a better way to say it is: Jesus *is* God come *to* us.

FOUR: Us

I'm well aware this may be jarring for you, but stay with me for a few more minutes, because if this is true, there are profound and far-reaching implications for how we think about evil, spirituality, and idolatry.

A word on each.

First off, evil.

One of the—if not *the*—primary objections that people have to the idea of God is this: *If there's a God and he's all-loving and all-powerful, why is there evil in the world?* Philosophers call this the "problem of evil," and it's a source of unbelief for millions of people. Note that: *millions*.

We just can't find a way to reconcile what we see on the news every day—ISIS and rape on campus and another young black man shot by the police on a routine traffic stop and a child eaten alive by an alligator in Florida—with the idea of a Creator God who is "compassionate and gracious."

But what's strange is the Scripture writers have little or nothing to say about the problem of evil, at least not in the philosophical sense.[48] They don't debate its nature or theorize about its origins or have a crisis of faith over a tsunami.

Why not?

Because evil was *assumed*.

Take, for example, Jesus' central prayer: "Your kingdom come, your will be done, on earth as it is in heaven."[49]

Notice that Jesus *assumed* that God's will was *not* done on earth. Hence, his prayer.

For Jesus, heaven is the place where God's will is done *all* the time. Earth, on the other hand, is the place where God's will is done *some* of the time. Because on earth, there are other "wills" at play. God isn't the only one with a will—an agenda for what he wants to see happen in the world, and the capacity to carry it out.

Human beings have a measure of free will as well.

And make sure you're paying attention here: *so do spiritual beings*.

You could even argue that nature has a "will" of its own.

That's a lot of wills . . .

God's will.

My will.

My friends', family's, coworkers', neighbors', and a few other billion human beings' wills.

Satan and his demonic armada's will.

Even nature's will.

All living in God's good, *free* world. Some under God's life-giving authority, others in flat-out rebellion.

To clarify, it's not that God's will is weak—on an even playing field with all the other wills. As if we, God, and Satan are all equal players in a game for the world. It's that in the universe God has chosen to actualize, love is the highest value, and love demands a choice, and a choice demands freedom. So God has chosen to limit his overwhelming capacity to override any "will" stacked against him, in order to create space for real, genuine freedom for his creatures, human and nonhuman. And evil is the by-product of that freedom that God built into the fabric of the universe. Put simply, God is incredibly good, but the world is a terrifyingly free, dangerous, beautiful place to call home.[50]

If I lost you there or upset you, that's okay. I get worked up about this too. This is an area of widespread disagreement in the global, historic church. It's complex. Everybody agrees that God is King and his creatures are free. But nobody agrees on what exactly "free" means; it's hard to work out. Some followers of Jesus give more place to God's control over the universe, while others emphasize his creatures' free will and autonomy.

Beware of anybody who claims to have it all figured out. There's a *lot* of mystery here, and we need to respect that.

But in my experience as a pastor, when people interpret the bad events of their lives, they rarely give place for the free will of *human* beings, much less *spiritual* beings. And in my opinion, to the degree that we ignore Satan and his friends' power and authority in the world, we end up attributing *his* evil to God.

That's a crisis of faith just waiting to happen. The reality is, planet Earth is the site of a cosmic war. So *of course* there's evil. You live in a battlefield. There's collateral damage all over the place. The Scripture writers just *assumed* that the universe is full of real spiritual beings who have a degree of power to animate evil empires, unleash injustice, stop the answer to prayers, shape "natural" disasters, even take over people's minds and bodies to carry out their dark agendas.

One theologian says it like this: "When one possesses a vital awareness that in between God and humanity there exists a vast society of spiritual beings who are quite like humans in possessing intelligence and free will, there is simply no difficulty in reconciling the reality of evil with the goodness of the supreme God . . . *it virtually sidesteps the problem of evil.*"[51]

Now, that last line is a bit of an overstatement. Please don't misread me. I'm *not* saying, "Something bad happened in your life? Oh, that was Satan."

All I'm saying is we need to get back to the worldview of Jesus and his Hebrew writer friends. Because when our worldview became shaped more by secularism than by Scripture, we created a philosophical problem with no good solution.[52]

So when evil comes to smash in your door, don't have a crisis of faith, as if Yahweh is to blame. The odds are, he's not. Instead, grieve and lament and meet God in the place of pain. But then get up and join Jesus in his quest to turn evil around for good.

And above all, hope for the day when Jesus will return to *end evil once and for all*.

Secondly, spirituality. Or religion or whatever you want to call it.

I live in Portland, Oregon, the epitome of the new category of choice on a religious survey: "spiritual but not religious." In my city, if you ask somebody about God or church, they'll usually say, "I don't go to church or anything, but I'm spiritual." By "spiritual," most people just mean they value meaning and purpose, watch *Oprah*, take a yoga class once in a while, or practice mindfulness. But a growing number of people actually *are* "spiritual" in the true sense of the word—they are in relationship with a spirit.

If you're from a more conservative city, maybe people say, "I'm not sure about Christianity, but I believe in God."

I used to nod my head, smile, and change the topic. But now I ask the follow-up question:

"You're spiritual? Cool. Who are you spiritual *with*?

Or . . .

"You believe in God? That's great. *Which one?*"

I never deny that people's experience of spirituality isn't real. I never argue it's fake or they have an overactive imagination. Instead, I talk about how much better Jesus is than all the other options. How he is the embodiment of the one true Creator God who made each and every one of us. And how the other "gods"/spirits/whatever-you-want-to-call-them are dangerous.

This also means we need to be careful and discerning and stay on our toes when it comes to "spirituality." Tarot cards, palm readers, Ouija boards—this stuff is more popular than ever. A lot of people laugh it off as a joke. But what if it's not? What if at least *some* of it is legitimate?

A while back, a college kid from my church came to me all shook up. Her friend went to a palm reader, and the palm reader was able to predict the future. A few weeks later, the prophecy came to pass exactly as the fifty-bucks-an-hour psychic said it would.

But this girl had no category for that, because in her mind, all of that stuff was fake. A delusion. She was your classic Western secularized Christian. So it scared her to death.

When people go to a palm reader or mess around with tarot cards in the living room or bow down to an idol in India or chant in a Bahá'í temple in suburbia, and when those same people experience something vivid and tactile and real—it's not necessarily psychosis or a hallucination or make-believe.

They're spiritual, just not with the Spirit of Jesus. With *another* spirit.

Finally, let's talk for a moment about idolatry.

There are commands all over the Scriptures to stay as far away as possible from idolatry. We already read the second commandment, but the New Testament says the same thing, repeatedly.

Paul writes, "My dear friends, flee from idolatry."[53]

John follows up with, "Dear children, keep yourselves from idols."[54]

If you've been around the church for a while, the odds are you've sat through a sermon or two about idolatry, and the pastor said something to the effect of "an idol is anything that takes the place of God in your heart."

One preacher I love said this: "If anything becomes more fundamental than God to your happiness, meaning in life, and identity, then it is an idol . . . The human heart is indeed a factory that mass-produces idols."[55]

The idea here is that an idol is a good thing that becomes ultimate—it becomes *the* thing. The idolatry conversation becomes a *priorities* conversation. The task is to keep watch over "the idols of the heart."

Now, I absolutely agree that we need to watch our heart.

I just don't think that's what the writers of the Bible mean by idolatry.

At least, I don't think that's the *primary*, face-value meaning.

An idol isn't a "good thing that becomes ultimate"; it's a statue that represents some kind of real spiritual being. It serves as a go-between, a conduit, a place for the worshiper to meet with his or her "god."

Now, of course, some idols are just a hunk of rock or metal or wood that somebody carved to make a little cash, and when the worshiper bows down in front of it, *nothing happens at all*.

But other idols are portals to a relationship with a real spiritual being, and when the worshiper comes to pray or sacrifice or share a meal for the dead, something *happens*.

For example, Paul writes this to the followers of Jesus in first-century Corinth: "Do I mean then that food sacrificed to an idol is anything, or that an idol is anything? No, *but* the sacrifices of pagans are offered to demons, not to God, and I do not want you to be participants with demons."[56]

Notice that for Paul, the danger of idolatry isn't that your priorities are out of whack; it's that you end up in relationship with a demon.

Idolatry was a touchy and volatile issue in the early church. In the ancient Mediterranean, temples were at the center of all social life, as well as of business and commerce. You would do more than worship in a temple; you would make friends, eat meals, negotiate business deals, sign contracts, buy and sell, etc. So, if you became a follower of Jesus and had to step out of the temples, it really cost you.

In the Western world, this is a nonissue for most people. Temples are a relic you walk past on a history tour when on vacation in Greece. Of course, Eastern religions like Hinduism are gaining popularity, and with that comes the open worship of other "gods." I just took a break and walked down the street to a Thai place for dinner. There was an idol in the front window. But for the most part, it's easy to avoid temples.

But that doesn't mean I'm off the hook.

I do think there's a secondary meaning to the New Testament's warnings against idolatry, one that especially rings true in the modern world.

In a secular society, the "gods" become nonspiritual—money, sex, power, more followers on Twitter, flatter abs, anything that "takes the place of God in your heart."

The temples become shopping malls and sports stadiums and senate chambers.

Worship becomes the sacrifice of money or time or your health or your family or your virginity or whatever it costs you to get what you want out of life.

But here's what we need to remember: behind these nonspiritual, secular non-gods, there is often lurking a *real* spiritual being. Like with an idol, behind that hunk of wood or rock or metal is often a creature with a scary amount of power.

The New Testament scholar N. T. Wright says it this way: "When we humans commit idolatry—worshiping that which is not God as if it were—we thereby give to other creatures and beings in the cosmos a power, a prestige, an authority over us which *we*, under God, were supposed to have over *them*. When you worship an idol, whatever it is, you abdicate something of your own proper human authority over the world and give it instead to that thing, whatever it is."[57]

I can't help but think of our culture's obsession with sex, and the dark underbelly of hard-core porn and sex trafficking and child prostitution happening in our own cities.

You're telling me there's nothing demonic behind *that*?

Or I think of the rampant pursuit of money in the West, and the high cost of globalization. There are upward of twenty-eight *million* slaves in the world today. More than ever before. For a tiny fraction of the world to live in Western-style luxury, it takes hundreds of millions of people living under economic oppression, if not full-on slavery. Sure, your new shoes are great and only cost you fifty bucks. But they were made by a dirt-poor woman in Vietnam working twelve hours a day, seven days a week, just to survive.

You're telling me the nightmare that global trade has become is just bad business deals? Corrupt, money-hungry companies? That there's *no* demonic power at work here?

I wonder if it's the nonspiritual things in our secular world that are the most spiritually lethal. As the infamous Keyser Söze put it, "The greatest trick the devil ever pulled was convincing the world he doesn't exist."[58]

This is a bit different from the "idolatry" in the New Testament, but still, *all the more reason to stay away from it*. Money has enough lure and pull and sway all by itself. Sex is intoxicating and addictive. If we accidentally open up our lives to a demonic being behind money or sex or whatever our "god" of choice is, we're in that much more trouble.

So, to end.

We are created beings. That means we're hardwired for worship. Made by the Creator to love and live for something greater than ourselves.

Worship isn't a religious thing; it's a *human* thing.

Followers of Jesus worship.

Jews worship.

Muslims worship.

Hindus and Wiccans and Druids and neo-pagans and Mormons and Jehovah's Witnesses and tribal witch doctors worship.

And famous anti-god, secular atheists from Oxford worship.

We *all* make sacrifices. When you read about animal sacrifice in the Bible, keep in mind that in the ancient world, animals were currency—money over time.

What do you spend your money on?

What about that precious commodity we call time?

When you're in need or in trouble or in a rough spot, where do you go for an escape? To a sacred book or a temple or a yoga mat or a chant or a bottle or a gym or a website or a relationship?

Where do you look for meaning and significance that will outlast your short years on planet Earth?

We just can't stop worshiping, any more than we can stop breathing.

In his commencement address at Kenyon College, the novelist and social critic David Foster Wallace eloquently said, "In the day-to-day trenches of adult life, there is actually no such thing as atheism. There is no such thing as not worshiping. Everybody worships. The only choice we get is *what* to worship."[59]

He went on to warn that if you worship the wrong thing, it "will eat you alive."

Worship beauty and romance and sex . . . and you will always feel ugly and lonely, and when you age, you will die decades before your time.

Worship money and stuff and that extra car you don't need . . . and you will always feel poor and discontented and unhappy with the life you actually have.

So to say it again: there is one true Creator God who made the world and everything good, beautiful, and true in it. He and he alone is deserving of worship. He is the only source of life and peace and meaning and significance that will last past death and into forever.

Love him with all your heart and soul and strength, with every scrap of your being. Not Chemosh or Aphrodite or Shiva or Elvis or the new Audi or V-cut abs or a 4.0 or whatever "it" is for you.

Worship GOD.

Chapter 3

"The LORD [Yahweh], the LORD [Yahweh], **the compassionate and gracious God**, slow to anger, abounding in love and faithfulness, maintaining love to thousands, and forgiving wickedness, rebellion and sin. Yet he does not leave the guilty unpunished; he punishes the children and their children for the sin of the parents to the third and fourth generation."

God as Father and Mother, and his baseline emotion toward you: mercy

Imagine living in the ancient Near East in 1500 BC. You're a Hebrew, formerly a slave in Egypt, now traipsing through the desert around Mount Sinai.

You inhabit a spiritually charged universe of "gods" and "goddesses." And these divine beings are anything but nice. Read any ancient text. The gods were *mean*—finicky and capricious and ready to fly off the handle at the slightest infraction.

So you made sacrifices. Naturally. To keep the gods off your back. Or maybe to get the gods on your side. At first it was a bird or a goat. Then you ratchet up to a bull. But eventually they might ask for your child. Maybe even your firstborn.

Anybody remember History of World Civilization class from freshman year? Think of the story of Troy. It takes place around the same time as the story of Moses on Mount Sinai.[1] The Greek king Agamemnon is sailing across the Mediterranean to fight in the Trojan War, but his fleet is dead in the water, no wind. Because Artemis—the goddess of Greece—is angry.[2] She's *always* angry. She demands that he makes a brutal sacrifice—his daughter Iphigenia. So what happens? He does it, cutting her throat to appease Artemis's wrath.

And immediately, *the wind starts to blow*.

Myth or history?

Random weather patterns in a superstitious age? Or a cruel, malignant *elohim* at work?

Hard to tell.[3]

But if you live in the ancient world, you live in fear of the gods.

Then Yahweh—say it with me: *the one true Creator God!*—comes to your rescue. He saves you out of Egypt. Leads you through the Red Sea and across the desert. Gives you food and water to survive the journey. And you've done nothing to deserve any of it.

Who *is* this God?

This God is nothing like Artemis or Amun-Ra or Marduk. He tells you his name—Yahweh—coaxing you into relationship. Apparently he really wants to know and be known by you.

Then he tells you what he's like. And the *first* thing you learn is that he's "compassionate and gracious."

In the Hebrew Scriptures, order matters. Order is a clue as to what's most important. The fact that "compassionate and gracious" is at the top of the list of Yahweh's character traits means it's the dominant one—the *most important* thing there is to know about him.

Now, this phrase "compassionate and gracious" is *rahum we-hanun* in Hebrew.[4]

Can you say that?

Come on, give it a try . . .

Rahum we-hanun.

Well done.

Rahum we-hanun is a word pairing in Hebrew. Meaning, not only do these two words sound alike, but they are laid side by side to help explain each other.

Let's pull these two words apart, and then we'll put them back together.

First off, *rahum*, or "compassionate." It's usually translated "merci-ful."[5] It's from a root word meaning "female womb." The idea behind it is the feeling a mother has toward her infant child.

So Yahweh is a mother?

He has a womb?

He has *feelings*?

Kind of.

Here are a few examples of where *rahum* is used in the Scriptures . . .

In the history books, there's a quirky story about two women fight-ing over a child. Both claim they are the mother, but it's the ancient world and there's no DNA test, so King Solomon comes up with an ingenious plan: cut the baby in half and give it to both mothers. That should flush out the true parent. Immediately, the true mother "was deeply moved out of love for her son and said to the king, 'Please, my lord, give her the living baby! Don't kill him!'"[6]

In the original Hebrew, it reads that she was deeply moved by her *rahum*—her intense, visceral, motherly love for her child.

Here's another one: in the prophet Isaiah, Yahweh says, "Can a mother forget the baby at her breast and have no *compassion* on the child she has borne? Though she may forget, I will not forget you!"[7]

But one of my favorites is the Hebrew poetry. First the writer quotes Exodus 34v6:

> The LORD [Yahweh] is compassionate and gracious,
>> slow to anger, abounding in love.

Then he speaks to the *rahum* of Yahweh:

> As a father has *compassion* on his children,
>> so the LORD [Yahweh] has *compassion* on those who
>>> fear him.[8]

So *rahum* is how a parent *feels* about their children.

I watch my wife, Tammy, with our three kids. If there's so much as a single cry in the middle of the night, she's out of bed and by their side—usually before I even wake up.

She's *compassionate*.

Honestly, I'm not compassionate by nature, and to tell the truth, I'm not really a kid person—I'm quiet and orderly and, well, *neat*. But my three kids melt my heart to *butter*.

The other day, Moses—my six-year-old—asked if we could wrestle. R's are hard for Mo, so "wrestle" becomes "westle." I was in my office answering an email and said, "Sorry, Moses, not now. Daddy's busy."

But then he said, "If I kiss you, *then* could we westle?"

Five seconds later, we were on the floor laughing and kicking around like kung fu masters.

When it comes to my kids, I'm *compassionate*. I feel a deeply rooted love and affection for Jude and Moses and Sunday.

And this is just a glimpse, a faint echo of how Yahweh feels about *his* kids. About you. And me.

Tragically, for some of you this doesn't connect at all. Your family of origin is so warped out of shape that you have no idea what a compassionate parent is like. Your dad was always mad at you, just waiting for you to screw up. Or your mom was the archetypal perfectionist—always nagging at you, critical and condescending. You were never smart enough. Athletic enough. Pretty enough. *Good* enough. Or maybe your parents just weren't around. You grew up on your own. So the idea of Yahweh as a parent doesn't resonate.

But for others of you, this taps into a deep part of your soul. Especially if you're a parent yourself. You know there is no love as fierce as that of a mother or father for a child. The love of a man for a woman, of a soldier for their country, of a sports fan for their team—*none* of it comes even *close* to the love of a parent for their kids. It's this emotive, visceral, in-the-marrow-of-your-bones kind of love that is stronger that life itself.

And it's how God feels about you.

Pause for a moment.

Let that sink in . . .

So, *rahum*, or "compassion," is a *feeling* word.

In contrast, "gracious" is an *action* word. In Hebrew, it's *hanun*. It means "to show grace" or "to show favor." It's something you do. It has this idea of help. To *hanun* somebody is to help them out in a time of need.

For example, *hanun* is used in *Exodus*: "If you take your neighbor's cloak as a pledge, return it by sunset, because that cloak is the only covering your neighbor has. What else can they sleep in? When they cry out to me, I will hear, for I am *gracious*."[9]

So here, "gracious" has to do with interest rates on a loan. It's justice for the poor. It's a coat to keep you warm at night.

The word pops up again in *2 Kings*: "Hazael king of Aram oppressed Israel throughout the reign of Jehoahaz. But the LORD [Yahweh] was *gracious* to them and had *compassion* and showed concern for them."[10]

Here, "gracious" is saving Israel from annihilation by a foreign army. It's a wall of defense around an embryonic nation.

Then it shows up in *Psalms*. The poet quotes Exodus 34:

> You, Lord, are a compassionate and gracious God,
>   slow to anger, abounding in love and faithfulness.

Then comes a prayer:

> Turn to me and be *gracious* to me;
>> give your strength to your servant,
>> and save the son of your maidservant.[11]

Here, a prayer for God's "grace" is a prayer for God to rescue and save Israel out of danger. For the God-who-responds to *do something*.

So, to recap: "compassionate" is a *feeling* word. Yahweh is like a father, or even a mother, and we're like his children. And "gracious" is an *action* word. It means, like a parent, God comes to the rescue when his kids need help.

These two words link up and fuse together to show us what Yahweh is like: he's compassionate and gracious.

When we come before God—in morning prayer or in worship at church or on our afternoon run or in the middle of a crisis at work—we come before a God who *feels*, who cares about us. *And* a God who *acts*, who wants to help, to do something about our situation.

As I see it, there are three basic ways people come before God . . .

The first is **based on what we've done.**

It sounds like this: "God, I'm a good person. I go to church. I volunteer. I even give money. So would you ____?"

We're back to the math formula. The implicit idea here is that God *owes* you. This game rarely works with God. The only thing that can effectively keep you from God's mercy is thinking you deserve it. This is one of the many reasons that religious people are often the farthest from God.

The second way is **based on what's been done to us**, or our circumstances.

Maybe you're in a rough spot. Life's not going well. You need help. So your prayer sounds something like this: "God, it's really hard right now. I'm going through hell. How could you let this happen to me? It's not fair. So would you ____?"

We play the victim card. Trying to show God how badly we need his mercy, trying to manipulate God to get what we want.

And there's a time and a place to pray like this. To lament. To protest all that's wrong about your life.

But there's a better way forward, a third way to come before God: not based on what you've done or what's been done to you, but **based on who God is—based on his mercy**.

In this posture, prayer sounds something like this: "God, you are compassionate—you care about me. And you're gracious—you help. And God, you don't owe me a thing, and there's a ton of other people who have it way worse than I do, but based on your mercy, I ask for you to ____."

Now, once again, prayer isn't a formula. There's no "right" way to pray, but Yahweh seems to find this kind of prayer far more compelling than anything else.

But is this how you and I approach God?

Or not?

Okay, let's keep going. All this talk about how nice Yahweh is sounds warm and fuzzy, but there's a disturbing side to the mercy of God . . .

TWO: Stories

There's a lot of violence in the Bible. Obviously. The ancient world was a barbaric, cruel place. (As if it's not anymore?) And Yahweh, as always, was way ahead of his people, coaxing them forward to a world where you love your enemy, not behead them. But that's a long journey, and we read a lot of bloody war stories along the way. The kind of stories that atheists blog about and fundamentalists yell about and most of us just skip over and pretend like it's not a problem.

These stories are a challenge. There's no way around that. They are hard to reconcile with the character of Yahweh and the teachings of Jesus.

But there's an even greater challenge—all the stories about God's *mercy*. There are even more of those. In the middle of all the blood and gore, Yahweh—the compassionate and gracious God—is constantly at work to rescue and save.

We need to keep these stories alive.

Here's one: it's about a prophet named Jonah. Some people think it's history; others think it's more of an allegory. Either way, it's a great story. In the opening line of Jonah's autobiography, we read that the word of Yahweh came to Jonah son of Amittai: "Go to the great city of Nineveh and preach against it, because its wickedness has come up before me."

Nineveh was the capital of the Assyrian Empire. Assyria was the dominant empire of the day and the archenemy of Israel. They'd been at war with the Hebrews on and off for centuries. And the Ninevites were the stuff of legend. A few decades ago, archaeologists found a Ninevite library. Their writings are *crazy*.

Speaking of a city he just destroyed, King Shalmaneser II had this to say: "A pyramid of heads I reared in front of his city. Their youths and their maidens I burnt up in the flames."

So he made a giant pile of heads by the front gate and burned the women and children alive. Yet another reason for the Geneva Convention.

His son, Sennacherib, had this to say about a king he defeated: "I flayed [him], his skin I spread upon the wall of the city."[12]

On the top ten list of things you *don't* want to happen if you're an ancient king: getting skinned alive.

One of Sennacherib's descendants, King Ashurbanipal, was true to the family name. Writing about another king, and another war, he said, "I pierced his chin with my keen hand dagger. Through his jaw . . . I passed a rope, put a dog chain upon him and made him occupy . . . a kennel."[13]

These were *not* nice people.

If you're Jonah, Nineveh isn't exactly a place you want to plant a church. Which is why the next line reads tells us that Jonah ran away from the Yahweh and headed for Tarshish.[14]

Nineveh was to the east, a few days walk.

Tarshish was to the west, across the ocean, on the edge of Spain. It was literally the last city on the map in the ancient world. The Hebrew equivalent of Timbuktu.[15]

So Jonah runs in the *exact opposite* direction—to the last vestige of civilization. But notice that odd line in the story. As terrifying as the Assyrians were, he's not running from Nineveh; he's running from *Yahweh*. Why? We don't find out until the end of the story.

After a run-in with a storm and a fish with digestive issues, Jonah finally ends up in Nineveh.[16] He goes around the city preaching a one-sentence message: "Forty more days and Nineveh will be overthrown."[17]

That's it. No three-point sermon. No cute story about his kids. No altar call. *One* sentence: Yahweh is going to kill all of you.

But in a shocking twist, the Ninevites repent! They turn away from the worship of other gods and the violence and injustice that come as a result; they turn to the worship of Yahweh, the Creator. Even the king repents. He calls for a day of mourning, and the people put on sackcloth and beg for Yahweh's mercy. Then we read, "When God saw what they did and how they turned from their evil ways, he relented and did not bring on them the destruction he had threatened."[18]

The word *relented* is *naham*ed in Hebrew. Remember that word? It means he "changed his mind."[19] Why? Because—you know what I'm going to say here—God *responds.* There's an elasticity to his dealings with people. He was going to destroy the Ninevites, but when he saw genuine repentance, he had mercy and changed his mind and the city went on to enjoy a long life.

But that's when the story gets even *more* interesting . . .

You would think Jonah would explode with joy, right? He had front-row seats to one of the greatest moves of God in human history. But instead, he goes into the adult equivalent of a temper tantrum.

He vents to Yahweh: "This is what I tried to forestall by fleeing to Tarshish." His worst fears have come to pass.

And then—wait for it!—he quotes Exodus 34 back to God!

"*I knew that you are a gracious and compassionate God, slow to anger and abounding in love*, a God who relents from sending calamity. Now, LORD [Yahweh], take away my life, for it is better for me to die than to live."[20]

Ha! This is *so* good!

Jonah is mad, seething with anger at Yahweh. Why? Because Yahweh was compassionate and gracious *to his enemies*. Because God, by nature, "relents from sending calamity"—he *nahams*; he responds to all sorts of people.

Here's the point of the story: we all love that God is compassionate and gracious with *us*. Or with our friends.

But what about when he's merciful to our enemies? To people who skin our kings like an animal hide and burn our women alive and carry off our children into slavery?

What about when God shows mercy to people who hurt us, stomp on us, gossip behind our back, lie about us to the boss, betray us, divorce us, and abandon us?

What about when God is merciful to *them*?

That's the problem with this God Yahweh—you just can't trust him to keep back blessing from people who don't deserve it. He goes around blessing all sorts of unsavory characters. People who aren't religious or spiritual or even *good*.

Because he's compassionate and gracious *to everybody*.

Most of us want mercy for ourselves—and justice for everybody else. But it doesn't work like that. God shows mercy to *all*.

I've only been deeply hurt twice in my life. Both times it was by a close friend. There are two sides to every story, but from my point of view, they were in the wrong. I did my best to patch things up, but they weren't even sorry. No repentance. Not even an apology. Just betrayal and pain.

The first time was hard, but not long after our relationship meltdown, his life fell apart, and mine actually went really well, so I got over it.

But the second time was much harder, because after we went our separate ways, he started saying nasty things behind my back, twisting the truth. I became the bad guy. A number of people left our church over untrue rumors. And it hurt, *deeply*.

But are you ready for the worst part? He did *really* well. I mean, the hand of God was all over his life. Blessing him at every turn.

I was so angry! It felt unfair, like an injustice. *God, how could you?* It was brutal for me to work through emotionally, but in the end, I came to realize something about God that I'll never forget: *that's just what God is like—compassionate and gracious*. He goes around blessing all sorts of people who don't deserve it.

And *I'm* living proof of that.

The odds are, so are you.

Who am I to think I "deserve" God's blessing any more than the next guy? In hindsight, I see all sorts of areas where I blew it in that relationship. My innocence was a myth. I was no victim. And the way I finally achieved peace was by daily coming back to the recognition that it's *all* mercy.

Now, Yahweh is also just, and he does get angry. We'll talk about that later. For now, know that his baseline emotion toward you is mercy.

THREE: Jesus

We see this all over the teachings of Jesus. One of Jesus' most disturbing and unpopular teachings was on nonviolence and enemy love:

"You have heard that it was said, 'Love your neighbor and hate your enemy.' But I tell you, love your enemies and pray for those who persecute you."[21]

Thousands of years later, we *still* can't quite grapple with the intensity of this statement. It's one thing not to kill our enemy, but to *love* them? This is especially hard in the US, where our comfort level with military violence is so high. After all, we're the "good guys." Even *Christians*—in particular, American Christians—have a really hard time with Jesus' teachings on enemy love. A lot of Americans would prefer to bomb our enemies or waterboard them or call in a drone strike.

Anything but *love* them.

Jesus' teachings on love for one's enemy are more subversive than ever before. But for Jesus, this isn't an abstract idea; it's a concrete reality grounded in Yahweh's character.

He goes on to say that "your Father . . . causes his sun to rise on the evil and the good, and sends rain on the righteous and the unrighteous."[22]

Remember, this was written to an agrarian society where the sun and rain were gifts from God. Jesus is essentially saying that every time the sun comes up and the rain comes down, that's God loving his enemies. Because God, by nature, is merciful.

This language of mercy is used all over the Gospels, which makes sense because Jesus is the compassionate and gracious God walking around as the rabbi from Nazareth.[23]

In Luke 17, ten men with leprosy come to Jesus and "lifted up their voices, saying, 'Jesus, Master, have *mercy* on us!'"[24]

In Luke 18, a blind man is begging on the side of the road. When Jesus comes within earshot, the man "calls out, 'Jesus, Son of David, have *mercy* on me!"[25]

In Matthew 17, a little boy is under the control of a demon. He's suffering from epilepsy and self-abuse. His father, desperate for healing and freedom for his son, falls on his knees before Jesus and prays, "Lord, have *mercy* on my son."[26]

In story after story, people come to Jesus, beg for mercy, and go away healthy and free.

But Jesus isn't just healing people because he's nice. A lot of people think of Jesus as the first-century equivalent of Mr. Rogers, the happy man with a shoe obsession. And while I'm sure Jesus was a delight to be around, he also got angry. Really angry at times.

Jesus' mercy doesn't come from a laid-back personality; it's born out of his character. *Yahweh's* character.

The most famous story Jesus ever told was about a father and his two sons.[27]

One son is a wild, brash party animal.

The other is a self-righteous snob.

The wild son asks for his inheritance early, which, in an ancient honor/shame culture, is the ultimate act of dishonor. He's essentially asking his dad to hurry up and die. In a shocking twist, the dad (who you quickly figure out is a picture of Yahweh) says yes, and the narcissistic son "set off for a distant country and there squandered his wealth in wild living."[28] Meanwhile, the older brother stays at home to be a good boy and work the field.

Naturally, the profligate son runs out of money, and his life goes belly-up. He lands in abject poverty—eating pigs' food, the end of the rope for a Jewish kid. Finally he comes to his senses and decides to go back home and beg his dad for mercy.

But when he gets close to home (and if this was a movie, the next part would happen in slow motion), "his father saw him and was filled with *compassion* for him; he ran to his son, threw his arms around him and kissed him."**29**

Usually we read the story as if it's about the two sons.

But what if it's actually about the father?

The son has done *everything* imaginable to break his father's heart, but the father's compassion is unshakable.

And get this: this is Jesus' view of God.

For Jesus, God is a merciful parent who feels deeply for his children. The kind of dad who sees his wayward son on the horizon and goes running out to meet him because he just can't wait another minute to wrap his son up into his chest.

Jesus had a name he used for God over and over again: *Father*.

For Jesus, the primary way we relate to God is not as a puny mortal cowering before an angry, malignant deity in the sky. But as sons and daughters in Daddy's lap—in trust, in vulnerability and intimacy, in relationship and love.

FOUR: Us

Now, let's take a deep breath and finish strong.

As I said before, **_who God is_ has staggering implications for who we are**.

There's a deeply Hebrew idea that goes all the way back to Moses on Mount Sinai. In the oldest rabbinic writings on Exodus 34v6–7, the rabbis talk about the "imitation of God." How it's Israel's job to "image" God—to copy and emulate and mimic what God is like to the world. The way the world is supposed to know what God is like is by looking at the people of God.

So Exodus 34 isn't just ground zero for a theology of God; it's also a manifesto for how God's people are to live.

God is compassionate, so we're to be compassionate.

God is gracious—we should be too.

There's a symbiotic relationship between a Father and his sons and daughters. A family. DNA.

We see this in the teaching on enemy love that we read a few pages back. Notice Jesus' rationale for why we are to love our enemies: "Love your enemies and pray for those who persecute you, *that you may be children of your Father* in heaven."[30]

The word *children* can be translated "heirs." Not only are we God's children, but we're God's heirs—the royal children of King Yahweh himself. And the family name is at stake. It's our job, our responsibility, to carry the family's honor. To represent our Father to the world.

In Luke's version of the story, Jesus adds on, "Be merciful, just as your Father is merciful."[31] It's the kind of landmark statement with a resonance and vibration and echo to it.

The world needs more mercy. A lot more. We have plenty of blog posts and op-eds and talking heads, and there's a place for that, but what we really need are sons and daughters of the Father to go out and show his mercy to the world.

Mercy is one of those things you just can't ever have enough of.

For some of you, this is your gift. Literally. In *Romans*, Paul writes that "if your gift . . . is to show mercy, do it cheerfully."[32] Some of you are *so* dang good at this—it's like you have an uncanny talent for mercy. I think of my wife. Tammy is compassionate and gracious by nature. It's hardwired into her personality. She's empathy on legs. People will come up to her in the most random places— usually in line at Whole Foods or when we're running late for an appointment—and just *dump* all their deepest, darkest secrets on her. She has an incredible gift.

Me, on the other hand—well, I *don't* have that gift.

Part of it is just my personality—I'm type A, task-driven, impatient.

I think fast and move faster. So in my weaker moments, I can easily come off as curt or dismissive.

Or as Jesus would say, *unmerciful*.

But it also has to do with my view of God. Oh, I know that God is "compassionate and gracious." I mean, I'm writing a book on it, right? I know this. But at a subconscious level, part of me still feels like God is angry with me. Like I'm a frustration or a disappointment or a screw-up and I need to earn his love.

Maybe it's my soft-fundamentalist church upbringing. Maybe it's a traumatic event from my childhood that my therapist has yet to unearth. Maybe it's just my personality—me projecting my own wiring onto God. I don't know. But it's there, in my gut.

I live with this nagging sense that I need to:

Get my act together.

Work harder.

Do more.

Be better.

Earn my keep.

Take it up a notch.

And quit screwing around.

Where does this feeling come from? Not from God.

Slowly but surely, I'm learning—or should I say *re*-learning—that God is merciful. Most of my education has been in a graduate program called fatherhood. Nine years ago, when my first son was born, I finally started to understand how God feels about me. Jude had done nothing but cry and poop and cost money and steal my wife's sanity and keep me up all night, *but I couldn't. stop. kissing. him*. I was a fire hydrant with a blown cap—a torrent of loving emotions all dumping out of my heart.

And this is from *me*—Mr. Type A.

Can you imagine how *God* feels about his children?

So to wrap up: at Bridgetown Church, I like to end my teachings with questions. Jesus would frequently do that—leave his audience with questions instead of answers.

So here are a few that come to mind . . .

Who are your enemies? The people who abuse you, stomp on you, trash-talk you, drive the knife a little deeper, make your life a living hell? The people you hate?

What would it look like for you to show mercy to them? Even *love* them?

Start with this: forgive them.

But they're not even sorry? Doesn't matter. Release them from your thirst for justice.

Then pray for them. And don't pray for a flat tire or bankruptcy or their plane to go down in a freak tornado over Southern California or them to go on an important date only to realize later they have a rogue nose hair stretching down their chin. Ahem. No. Even though you want to pray for justice, pray for *mercy*. For blessing.

And get ready for God to answer it.

Next, who are the people you have daily opportunities to show mercy to? The people you rub shoulders with? The people at the office, gym, church, and home who need mercy?

Hint: they are usually the people who annoy you the most . . .

If you have a wedding band on your fourth finger, then it's your spouse. Marriage is the art of learning to forgive over and over and *over* again. Marriage only works when nobody is keeping score. When nobody "wins" or "loses." When every day is a chance to give and receive mercy.

When your spouse screws up—and they will—when they forget to put the recycling bin out on Monday night or pay the electric bill on time or when they talk with a mouth full of burrito or do some-thing to annoy you—do you show mercy?

By the way, we don't get to self-evaluate. This is the kind of question you ask your *spouse*.

I just asked Tammy if she thinks I'm merciful. Want to know what she said? "Not really." But then she said each year I get a little better. A little more compassionate. A little more gracious. I guess that's what following Jesus is all about.

If you're a parent, then every day you have a chance to show mercy. Parents, one of the most important jobs you have is to show your kids the character of Yahweh. If you love them well, it will make it that much easier for them to believe in a God who is compassionate. But if you're cranky and always biting their little heads off, and then you tell them God is their "Father," don't expect it to sink in.

One of the greatest gifts you can give your children is to raise them so that they have as little *unlearning* to do as possible when they grow up. Especially about God.

Or maybe you don't have kids, or even a spouse. You're single. Maybe for you it's your roommate or sibling or friend.

Here's the thing: *difficult people are never hard to find*. There's plenty to go around. You probably have one on your street or in your apartment building or at the office or in your church. If not, there's always the holidays with that weird uncle . . .

Who has God put in your life—to frustrate you and rub you the wrong way?

Listen: every time you see them, every time they annoy you or upset you or make you mad, it's an opportunity to be like God, to show mercy.

Don't miss it.

Finally, do you honestly believe that God is your Father? Do you believe this to be true in the deepest part of your being? That God is like a parent. He *feels* compassion for you. He's gracious. He wants to help.

Is this how you relate to God? Do you come to him in trust and freedom and intimacy and anticipation—like a child to his mom or dad?

If not, there's no time like the present. I mean that. Right now, sitting there reading this book, you can come before God.

There's an allusion to Exodus 34 in the New Testament book of *Hebrews*: "Let us then approach God's throne of grace with confidence, so that we may receive *mercy* and find *grace* to help us in our time of need."[33]

Hear the echo from Mount Sinai there?

This is a claim about how we are to approach God, and I love the writer's choice of words—*with confidence*. We're to approach the God who speaks worlds into existence *with confidence*. Because he's our Dad. We come to his "throne of grace," not as beggars off the street, but as his sons and daughters—royal heirs to the kingdom.

When I get home from work, my kids don't bow down and crawl up to kiss my feet. Sadly. They run and *jump* into my arms—"Daddy!"

Confidence. *That's* how we are to come to God.

So where do you need mercy?

Where do you need grace to help in time of need?

Put this book down.

Go to the Father.

Like the kid you are.

Appeal to his compassion. Ask for his grace.

No matter where you've been or what you've done recently, even with the stink of the pigsty still on your breath, the Father is already running toward you—arms spread open, smile wide. And the cooks in the kitchen are busy gearing up for the party.

Chapter 4

"The LORD [Yahweh], the LORD [Yahweh], the compassionate and gracious God, **slow to anger**, abounding in love and faithfulness, maintaining love to thousands, and forgiving wickedness, rebellion and sin. Yet he does not leave the guilty unpunished; he punishes the children and their children for the sin of the parents to the third and fourth generation."

Why we actually crave the wrath of God

Okay, we just hit the halfway mark. Well done. I feel like we're getting somewhere, and the best is yet to come.

For this chapter, first we'll talk about human anatomy,

then Daniel Day Lewis,

then an obscure Hebrew prophet,

then axis points, bumper stickers, Jesus kicking over tables,

and finally, what it all means for tomorrow morning when we get out of bed.

Sound like a plan? I hope so . . .

Next up on the list is "slow to anger."

This is a fun one. In Hebrew, it's *erek apayim*, and it literally means "long of nostrils."

True story. Not making this up. God's nostrils are *loooong*, believe you me.

Contrary to popular opinion, there is no such thing as a literal, word-for-word translation of the Bible. It's impossible to directly translate one language into another, especially an ancient Semitic language like Hebrew into modern English.[1] But "slow to anger" does a great job of capturing the meaning behind this ancient word picture.

Think about what happens when you lose your temper: your chest sucks in a gulp of air and your nostrils flare out as you verbally unload on your victim.

But . . .

If you're *slow* to anger, when you get mad, you shut your mouth, purse your lips, and breathe in through your nose.

You're *erek apayim*.

Long of nostrils.

Slow to anger.

This phrase is used twice in a collection of ancient Hebrew wisdom sayings called *Proverbs*. In each example, we learn more about this aspect of Yahweh.

In Proverbs 14, we read:

> Whoever is *erek apayim* has great understanding,
>   but one who is quick-tempered displays folly.[2]

Here, the antonym of slow to anger is "quick-tempered"—you get mad quickly and easily.

There's a similar maxim in Proverbs 16:

> Whoever is *erek apayim* is better than the mighty,
>   and he who rules his spirit than he who takes a city.[3]

In this verse, the synonym for slow to anger is "rules his spirit," or what we call self-control. If you're slow to anger, it's not that you don't have feelings of frustration; it's that you don't lose it and explode when you get worked up emotionally; you have control over your feelings of frustration and anger and even rage.

So here's the basic idea: **you can make God mad, but you really have to work at it.**

Now, there are two sides to this part of Yahweh's character . . .

On the one hand, God is *slow* to anger.

Unlike the other "gods," Yahweh doesn't have a temper. He's not volatile or edgy or spasmodic. He doesn't fly off the handle or slam the door and storm out of the house in the God version of a temper tantrum.

When the Hebrew Bible was translated into Greek, the Hebrew scholars translated *erek apayim* with a Greek word meaning "patient." Actually, the earliest English translations used the word *long-suffering*. That's even better. It does a great job of capturing the idea. Yahweh is patient, long-suffering.

There was another ancient translation of the Hebrew Bible called a Targum. It was a translation into Aramaic—probably the language Jesus grew up speaking. This translation was more of a paraphrase—they were free and limber with the original Hebrew. But I love how they translated Exodus 34: God is "patient, the One who makes anger distant and brings compassion near."[4]

In this reading from around the time of Jesus, Yahweh's anger is *far away*, but his compassion is *close by*.

Kind of like Daniel Day Lewis.

Didn't see *that* coming, did you?

Anybody seen the movie *Lincoln*? Lewis's performance in that film is incredible. I love the scene where the president is with his Cabinet at a late-night meeting in the White House. He wants to pass the Thirteenth Amendment and put an end to the plague of slavery, but his entire team is against him. Every single member.

He's the solitary voice. There's a dramatic moment where his Cabinet is yelling at each other like hormone-heavy teenagers, but Lincoln is just sitting there at the head of the table, quiet and calm. The infighting gets nasty and keeps ratcheting up until, finally, he *slams* his fist on the table and *yells*, "I can't listen to this anymore!"

A hush falls over the room. Because anger is *so* far out of character for him. As you can imagine, they all shut up and listen.

I love that, because when Lincoln finally lets out his anger, it's on purpose, deliberate, and under control. And it's fitting. It's the right emotional response.

I think that moment does a great job of capturing "slow to anger."

I'm not sure how you imagine God, but if you think of him as mercurial and ready to zap you with lightning the second you blow it, that's just not what God is like. At all.

God is *slow* to anger.

But on the other hand, God is slow to *anger*.

He does get mad. *Really* mad at times. This is something we don't like to talk about, but we need to.

A lot of people today have abandoned the idea of an angry deity in the sky as a hangover from a premodern, superstitious age. But the Scriptures speak of God's "wrath" more than *six hundred times*.

Here are a few samples . . .

In *Psalms*, we read:

> God is a righteous judge,
>> a God who displays his *wrath* every day.
> If he does not relent,
>> he will sharpen his sword,
>> he will bend and string his bow.[5]

God has a sword? A bow? A weapons depot? Maybe that's why the prophet Habakkuk prays, "In *wrath* remember mercy."[6]

You don't want to get on God's bad side.

King David says this about God:

> You *hate* all who do wrong;
>> you destroy those who tell lies.
> The bloodthirsty and deceitful
>> you, LORD [Yahweh], *detest*.[7]

Or in another poem:

> Yahweh examines the righteous,
>> but the wicked, those who love violence,
>> he *hates* with a passion.[8]

God hates?

He detests people?

But I thought God is love.

Well, notice *who* God hates—the "wicked" and "those who love violence." Imagine the terrorist in a shopping mall with bombs strapped to his chest, the con artist ripping off the elderly widow, the corrupt politician, the abusive father, the date rapist who gets off scot-free, the pedophile who gets called "uncle."

When people say to me: I can't believe in a God of wrath,

I say: *Yes*, you can.

Every time you read about a child sold into prostitution by her family, every time you hear about yet another oil spill by a careless, greedy multinational corporation, every time you read about rape or murder or genocide, you think to yourself, *This isn't how it's supposed to be.*

You're right. It's *not* how it's supposed to be. It's not God's will. There's no secret plan behind all the injustice in the world. It's evil, plain and simple. "Gods" and human beings are at war with Yahweh. Yes, Yahweh has a plan to work all this mess into good, but he still feels the pain of war. Remember he's a *person*, not an idea. He has feelings. And he *feels* anger over evil in the world.

There are times when the healthy, emotionally mature response to evil is anger.

Here's my favorite definition of God's wrath: "his steady, unrelent-ing, unremitting, uncompromising antagonism to evil in all its forms and manifestations."[9]

Notice that God's anger is very different from *our* anger. At least, a lot of our anger. Let me sketch out a few examples . . .

Our anger is almost always from a wounded ego—somebody hurt us or made us feel stupid or took advantage of us or didn't do what we wanted. It's inherently selfish, even narcissistic.

But Yahweh's anger is from a parent-like love for his children, angry at a drug dealer for trying to sell dope to our children or at little Jonny for constantly running into the middle of the street.

Our anger is usually unjust. It's disproportionate to the offense. I think of the theologian Cornelius Plantinga's line, "All shots are return fire."[10] Meaning, human history is just an endless cycle of violence—he hit me, so I beat him to a pulp; he burned down my barn, so I killed his wife; they flew planes into our skyscrapers, so we invaded their country. Etc., etc. This is where the command in the Torah of "eye for eye, tooth for tooth" was millennia ahead of its time.[11] The natural tendency when somebody gives you a black eye is to give them *two* black eyes. We say we want justice, but usually we want revenge. Think of how much we love revenge movies, where somebody goes on a rampage. Somebody kidnaps Liam Neeson's daughter (now *that*, Mr. Neeson, was a fun film . . .), and what does he do in return? He kills, like, thirty men!**12** And we eat it up.

God's anger isn't like that; the punishment fits the crime. There's a justice we just can't match.

Our anger—or at least my anger—is quick to flare up. It's in a rush. It doesn't wait for the whole story to come out or to give a second chance. It's *im*patient.

Whereas Yahweh's anger is on tempo. Patiently waiting. It builds up to the right time and place.

So here's the ground we've covered so far: God does get angry, but it's unusual. His baseline is "compassionate and gracious, *slow to anger*."

TWO: Stories

Let's look at yet another story where Exodus 34v6–7 is quoted, and we see this idea play out. To do that, let's revisit the city of Nineveh, but this time with a prophet named Nahum.

As I said in the last chapter, Nineveh was the capital city of Assyria—a barbaric, oppressive empire stretching across the Middle East. Yahweh sent the prophet Jonah to warn the Assyrians of impending doom.

And in a bizarre twist, they *naham*ed. They repented.

But because Yahweh is a person and he *responds*, in turn he *naham*ed. He changed his mind and spared the city.

And the story ends on a semi-happy note. Jonah is off pouting, but the Ninevites are alive and well.

Fast-forward 150 years to the prophet Nahum. His book—a short, little-known writing appearing near the end of the Old Testament— takes place in the same city, a few generations down the line. Tragically, the Ninevites have turned back to evil. In context, they've just taken ten of Israel's twelve tribes into slavery, killing off God's people and leaving the north of Israel in a smoldering heap.

And Yahweh's patience has finally reached its limit. Nahum writes:

> The Lord [Yahweh] is a jealous and avenging God;
>> the Lord [Yahweh] takes vengeance and is filled
>>> with wrath.
> The Lord [Yahweh] takes vengeance on his foes
>> and vents his wrath against his enemies.
> The Lord [Yahweh] is *slow to anger* but great in power;
>> the Lord [Yahweh] will not leave the guilty unpunished.[13]

To clarify, that's a quote of Exodus 34v6–7.

Interesting. Exodus 34 gets quoted with reference to Nineveh *twice*. The first time after Yahweh spared the city. The second time when Yahweh has finally had enough.

Meaning what?

Meaning, Yahweh is compassionate and gracious and slow to anger—that's his *nature*; that's how he's wired. But there comes a time when God says, "Enough is enough. No more violence. No more injustice. No more killing and raping and stealing and enslaving. I've had it with evil. You're done."

There's a phrase used in the Scriptures about the "full measure" of sin.[14] It's usually used to describe why Yahweh delays his judgment. It's like God has a threshold. When sin crosses a line, his anger finally comes awake like a sleeping giant, and he puts a stop to it.

But here's what's fascinating about the Nineveh story: as far as we know, Nineveh was not destroyed by an "act of God"—a freak tsunami or citywide plague or fire from heaven; it was destroyed by Babylon, an up-and-coming world power to the south.[15] And by destroyed, I mean wiped out. To this day, there's nothing left but rubble.

You know any Ninevites?

Exactly.

Think about what this means. It means that the defeat of Nineveh by a pagan army is an example of Yahweh's "wrath."

Let's pull this apart: **you can plot Yahweh's wrath along four axis points—present, future, active, and passive**.

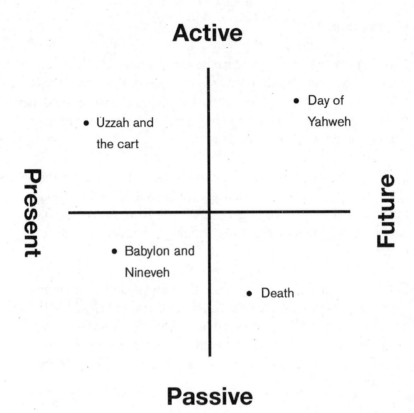

Active

Present • Uzzah and
the cart

• Day of
Yahweh

Future

• Babylon and
Nineveh

• Death

Passive

First, present and future . . .

Yahweh's **present wrath** is when he deals with evil now, on *this* side of judgment day, like he did with Nineveh. It's when he doesn't wait for a postmortem day of reckoning—he steps in *now* and stops evil dead in its tracks. It's when living, breathing people or even entire nations come under Yahweh's discipline and punishment.

But it's rare. It doesn't happen very often.

Yahweh's **future wrath** is when he deals with evil *later*, in what the Hebrew writers call the *day of Yahweh*, the day on the horizon when finally, after millennia of waiting, all the wrongs of human history will be undone.

As we know, the twentieth century was the bloodiest century on record. Why is that? Karl Marx said that "religion is the opium of the people."[16] For Marx, the way of Jesus was a foolish delusion. But years later, after living through the rise and fall of both Fascism and Communism and seeing the genocide and violence brought about by Marx's ideas, the Polish poet Czesław Miłosz argued that "the true opium for the people is belief in nothingness after death—the huge solace of thinking that for our betrayals, greed, cowardice, murders, we are not going to be judged."[17]

The modern world has it wrong: we *are* going to be judged.

But for the writers of the Bible, as well as teachers like Jesus, this cataclysmic "day of Yahweh" is a bad thing, *or a good thing*, depending on where you stand with God.

If you're the righteous—the man or woman in right relationships, with God, humanity, and the earth itself—then you *can't wait* for judgment. Especially if you're the oppressed. Finally, all the world will be set right.

But if you're the wicked, the oppressor, if you refuse Yahweh and his mercy, if you say no to his way of life—then this day should stand as a terrifying warning.

Because God isn't mean, but he is dangerous. Like gravity or nuclear power or a hurricane—you want to make sure you're on the right side of things.

Because God's future wrath is coming.

So, *present* and *future*.

Next, *active* and *passive*.

Active wrath is when God *acts*—directly—to put a stop to evil. It's like an invisible-but-real hand of God sweeps down in judgment.

There's a story in the Old Testament where the Israelites are moving the ark of the covenant to Jerusalem. The ark was this visible sign of the power and presence of Yahweh with his people. The most holy object in Israel's world. But they weren't taking it seriously. God told them to carry it on poles so they would never actually touch it. Instead they had it on a Philistine cart. Easier. Faster. Better. Right? But when the cart hit a pothole, a priest named Uzzah put out his hand to keep the ark from falling off the cart. And we read that Yahweh's "anger burned against Uzzah because of his irreverent act; therefore God struck him down, and he died there beside the ark of God."[18]

That's active wrath. You sin egregiously, and the next moment you're not breathing.

And don't think this is "just an Old Testament thing." There's a story in Acts 5 about the first followers of Jesus. A man lies to Peter (and God) about selling a property and giving all the money to the poor. And what happens? *He falls down dead on the spot.* Then, a few hours later, his wife comes in and tells the exact same lie, and *she* falls down dead. Romantic, no?

But here's what you need to understand: stories about God killing people get all the airplay—they're fodder for disenfranchised bloggers who are angry with the God they don't believe in. I get it. But there are *barely any* stories like that in the Bible. Active wrath is the exception to the rule. Most of the time, it's passive wrath.

Passive wrath is when God does *not* act, and *that is the judgment*. And this is how Yahweh usually deals with evil.

For example, in the Scriptures, God's judgment often looks like an invading army—Babylon coming to destroy Nineveh or, a few decades later, to destroy Jerusalem. But Babylon was the emerging world power—they would have gone to war against Nineveh and Israel with or without Yahweh's nudge. All God had to do was step back and remove his protection.

Even in my own nation's history, Abraham Lincoln said publicly that he thought the Civil War was God's judgment on America for slavery. In his second inaugural address, after asking how to reconcile the horror of war with the "divine attributes" of God—his answer was that the war would continue "until all the wealth piled by the bondsman's two hundred and fifty years of unrequited toil shall be sunk, and until every drop of blood drawn with the lash shall be paid by another drawn with the sword, as was said three thousand years ago, so still it must be said 'the judgments of the Lord are true and righteous altogether.'"[19]

What a fascinating theory on the Civil War. Let's say he was right: Did Yahweh make Americans kill each other? Not even remotely. He said, "Love your enemy." Love your fellow Americans goes without saying. The Civil War was outright, flagrant disobedience to the teachings of Jesus. But could it be that it was still an expression of God's wrath over slavery? I have no idea if Lincoln's hypothesis was right or wrong. But I do know it sounds a lot like the stories we read in Israel's history.

Now, to drag this from the history of nations down to you and me, God's passive wrath is when he doesn't act to keep us from evil. Usually it's when he lets us royally screw up our life.

In Paul's letter to the Romans, he writes about God's wrath over the downward spiral toward moral bankruptcy and social sabotage in first-century Rome. Notice, he keeps repeating this one phrase . . .[20]

"*God gave them over* in the sinful desires of their hearts to sexual impurity . . ."

"*God gave them over* to shameful lusts . . ."

"God gave them over to a depraved mind . . ."

There are times when God says, "Okay, have it your way." He takes away his hand of blessing and covering over your life, steps back, and says, "You're on your own now. Good luck."

And Nineveh is destroyed by Babylon.

And your body is torn apart by drugs.

The scandal breaks.

You get fired for cheating.

Your kids grow up to hate you.

Your marriage is wrecked by an affair.

For example, we think that when a guy gets caught in an affair, that's God's wrath. It's not. That's God's mercy. *God's wrath is when he gets away with it.* And his heart gets so warped out of shape that there's nothing left to ever give or receive love again.

If your heart is stubborn, cold, or in open rebellion against Yahweh, then the worst thing God can do is give you what you want and let all your desires come true.[21]

I know this is heavy, but stay with me. We're almost through the thick stuff.

To sum it up so far, Yahweh's wrath is:

present,

future,

active,

and passive.

But here's the eye-opening truth: most of God's wrath is either *present/passive* or *future/active*. Meaning, one day God will act decisively to put an end to evil forever. But in the meantime, God's way of dealing with sin is usually to step back and let it run itself into the ground.

It turns out that sin is its own punishment, and obedience its own reward.

Here's the salient point for this chapter: Yahweh waited for *150 years* before he gave Nineveh up! Honestly, if I was Yahweh—and thank God I'm not—I doubt I would have sent Jonah in the first place. But Yahweh gave the city chance after chance.

Because Yahweh is slow to anger.

Now, before we move on to Jesus, we need to clarify something. We live in a *very* different time than the second millennium BC. Our world is secularized to the core; most people are totally oblivious to the spiritual dimension of the universe. But Exodus 34 was written into a world teeming with "gods" and "goddesses," and as I said earlier, most of them were mean-spirited. To say they had anger management issues would be a gross understatement. Many of them were openly hostile and malignant, lurking in the shadows, just waiting for a chance to pounce.

It's in *this* kind of a world that Moses learns that Yahweh is compassionate and gracious, and *slow to anger*. This would have been an incredibly novel view of deity.

In fact, the Scripture writers' main problem with Yahweh's anger is that he doesn't get angry more often! They are far more frustrated with God's mercy than his wrath. They look out at the overwhelming amount of injustice in the world and vent their angst to God.[22] One of the most frequent prayers in the Bible is, "How long?"[23] The prophets, kings, politicians, farmers, and shepherds who write Scripture have no doubt that one day, Yahweh will bring evil to its logical conclusion. They just can't figure out, Why does he delay? Why does justice usually come in the *next* life, and not *this* one?

But we live in a radically different cultural milieu. For the most part, we have the exact *opposite* problem with Yahweh's anger. We were born in the middle of a tectonic shift in how Westerners think about God.

A lot of people have abandoned the "God is angry" narrative and simply replaced it with the exact opposite: "God is never angry at all."

As followers of Jesus, when we read these stories about Yahweh's anger or wrath or judgment, we feel like we need to apologize to our friends or explain it away or hide this socially unacceptable part of God away in the back room, as if Yahweh needs a little PR help to survive in the modern world.

The imagery of an angry God is passé. We've moved on, evolved to a more progressive world. It's time that we update Yahweh for the twenty-first century.

And with this move to recast God comes an even more discon-certing move to redefine love. For a lot of people, love has come to mean tolerance.

Think of the common slang in our culture:

"Hey, what's good for you is good for you."

"Who am I to judge?"

"Live and let live."

I can't help but think, *Really? Would you say that about an ISIS bomber? A deranged killer sneaking into an elementary school with a machine gun? A pedophile?*

I'm guessing *no*. So, clearly tolerance has a limit, even in our late-modern world. There's a line; we just disagree on where to draw it.

Keep in mind that there are two versions of tolerance. *Classic tolerance* is the idea that we can agree to disagree rather than kill each other or go to war over some petty thing. This was a revolutionary leap forward in social evolution. I'm all for it.

But *modern tolerance* is the much newer idea that right and wrong are elastic. In this view, to call out somebody's action as sin is to "judge" them. To disagree with somebody is to hate them. So, for example, if you disagree about sexuality, no matter how gracious and kind and intelligent you are, you immediately earn the label "bigot." But we all know that's ludicrous. To disagree with somebody *is just to disagree*. My wife and I disagree on a regular basis, but we love each other deeply.

My point is simply that love and tolerance are not the same thing.

The Nobel Peace Prize winner Elie Wiesel said, "The opposite of love is not hate, it's indifference."[24] At some point, tolerance starts to slide dangerously close to apathy.

Love—at least the kind of love Jesus talked about—often leads to anger. We get angry about things we care deeply about. Things we're passionate about.

This is the kind of anger we see in Yahweh. Anger that is patient, just, and unselfish—that comes out of a place of love. Anger that comes from a Father who cares about his kids.

In spite of all the current rebranding of God to fit the Western world, if we're going to take the Scriptures seriously, then we have to take this part of God seriously.

THREE: Jesus

Let's step forward to Jesus. Often this move to recast God as a progressive and love as tolerance is supposedly based on Jesus' teachings.

I recently heard a preacher say, "The message of Jesus was all-inclusive love."

Really?

The writer Mark's summary of Jesus' message is this: "The king-dom of God has come near. Repent and believe the good news!"[25]

Jesus' central, overarching message was that what he called the kingdom of God—the long-awaited age of peace and justice and healing for humanity and the cosmos itself—was finally breaking in through his life. That Yahweh was about to become king over the world and lead humanity into a glorious new stage of develop-ment. So we need to *repent*, to come over to his side, so that we can enter and enjoy his new reality.[26]

In fact, contrary to all the clichés about Jesus and love, Jesus says more about the coming judgment than *any* teacher in the New Testament. It was one of his major themes. He is constantly warning Israel, calling her to repentance in light of the coming day of Yahweh.

The caricature of Yahweh as the angry, violent "God of the Old

Testament" and Jesus as Mr. Rogers with a beard just doesn't hold up.

One story in particular does a profound job of capturing this reality. In it, Jesus goes to the temple in Jerusalem. For first-century Jews, the temple was the axis point between heaven and earth, a sacred space. But what Jesus finds there is beyond disturbing. The priests had become the aristocracy of the day and were in bed with Rome. The spiritual leaders of the nation had become corrupt. It's a tragic story that we've seen play out hundreds of times.

Here's what they did: you would come to the temple with say, a lamb, to sacrifice to Yahweh. Maybe you had to walk for two or three days just to get there from your village. You brought a good lamb, one of your best, because the Torah said the sacrifice had to be "without defect."[27] But the priest would inspect your lamb and say, "I'm sorry, but you're lamb isn't good enough. *But* . . . we just happen to have one for sale that's already been preapproved." And then he would sell it to you for a rip-off.

Or let's say you came from Rome or Alexandria—a much longer journey. Instead of a lamb, you would bring money to buy a sacrifice on-site in Jerusalem. I mean, who wants to walk hundreds of miles with a goat? It's not very fun. But when you got to the temple in Jerusalem, the money changers would say, "I'm sorry, but the priests don't take Roman currency here. You need to pay with the temple coin." And of course, they were the only bank in town, so they could charge an exorbitant exchange rate.

So what does Jesus do? He gets mad. *Really* mad. He makes a whip—true story—and starts chasing the money changers out of the temple, turning over tables, dumping money and animals on the ground, screaming at the religious establishment: "Get these out of here! Stop turning my Father's house into a market!"

The writer John has a great ending line to the story: "His disciples remembered that it is written: 'Zeal for your house will consume me.'"[28]

Is this how you picture Jesus? Whip in hand, fire in his eyes, knocking over tables and screaming at the money changers as they duck for cover and bolt for the parking lot?

This is one of those stories we skip in Sunday school . . .

I grew up in the 80s. Uh-huh. Anybody remember the flannelgraph?[29] This story never made it onto the flannelgraph. We had Jesus the Good Shepherd, and Jesus walking on water, and Jesus with the children—but we never had angry eyes Jesus with a weapon in his hand and spittle dripping off his chin.

Nope, never had that one.

But it makes sense. He's facing nauseating injustice. And he is livid. *How else is Jesus supposed to feel?* Anger is the mature, emotionally healthy response to this kind of corruption and gross defamation of Yahweh's name.

But here's what you need to see: this story happens at the end of Jesus' life, right before the cross.[30] In fact, it's one of the primary reasons that Jesus is put under arrest and then killed—you don't upset the status quo of the religious hierarchy and live. But Jesus has been to the temple dozens, if not *hundreds*, of times. He'd been coming there since he was a boy. It's not like he just walks in, sees the money changers' racket, and goes postal. Nothing about this story is spur of the moment. No, this is a thought-out, deliberate, on-purpose kind of anger.

A judgment. A reckoning. A line in the sand.

After *years* of calling Israel to repentance, Jesus says, "ENOUGH!"

This may be a very different Jesus from what you're used to. A Jesus who is loving, but still gets angry and isn't afraid to mete out judgment.

We need to live in the tension between love and anger. Most of us think of love and anger as incompatible. How can you love somebody *and* be angry at them? That just shows how much we still have to learn about love.

In Jesus we see that Yahweh's anger is *born out of his love*. The truth is, if you don't get angry occasionally, then you don't love. When you see somebody you love in pain, it should move you emotionally. And it should move you to action, to do something about it.

That's why Yahweh's love is an attribute, but his wrath isn't. The Scriptures teach that "God is love,"[31] but we never read "God is wrath." Wrath, or anger, is Yahweh's *response* to evil in the world.

The story about Jesus in the temple, clearing out the corrupt bureaucrats with a homemade whip, is a preview of what's to come, a glimpse over the horizon. There is coming a day when Jesus puts evil six feet under the ground. When the world is finally free. And it's because of Jesus' love, *and because of his wrath*, his passionate antagonism against evil in all its forms, that we can look forward to this glorious future.

FOUR: Us

I have no idea where you come from on the map—progressive or conservative, believer or agnostic, you love the Bible or you can't stand it. Obviously this is a thorny issue to talk about, and I'm sure I've upset some of you. But let's drag all this into our relationship to the Creator God.

Maybe you need to hear that Yahweh is *slow* to anger . . .

Maybe like me, you have this subconscious, nagging, in-the-back-of-your-head sense that God is just waiting for you to screw up so he can unload on you. The gun is cocked and you're in his crosshairs.

The odds are you grew up in a conservative, religious, "Christian" environment, or your personality is introspective and sensitive. Both are true of me.

Or maybe you grew up in an angry home and this vision of a God whose baseline feeling toward you is mercy—well, it sounds too good to be true. All you think of is your dad screaming at you from down the hall to pick up your room or else . . ..

Or maybe that's not you at all. You grew up way outside the walls of the church and come from a fine family. For you, it's that you just can't get your act together. There's a sin in your life—a bent toward what you know is wrong. It's like a rut in the road—no matter how hard you try, you keep slipping back and getting stuck in the mud. You're inching forward, but man, it's slow going. And you're scared that God is ticked at you.

All of you, please hear that God is *slow* to anger. He's patient. He sees your future—who you are *becoming*. And like a father, or even a mother, he's coaxing and calling you forward, one step at a time, into your destiny.

But maybe you need to hear that God is slow to *anger* . . .

You abandoned the idea of an angry Jesus years ago. You worship at the altar of tolerance and individualism. As our society drifts further into moral anarchy, it's no skin off your back. God, for you, is more like the permissive parent. You ever have a friend in high school whose parents were just chill? They let her drink, smoke pot, have sex with her boyfriend upstairs, skip school. They were "open-minded." I used to think, *Man, that's cool*. But now as a pastor dealing with the fallout of that kind of parenting in so many lives, I see the obvious truth: that's *not* cool, at all.

But is that how you imagine God? With a laissez-faire shrug at life?

Could it be that you value love as tolerance and even the progressive view of the world, in part because it gives you a free pass to do whatever you want? To be your own god?

Does not "judging" others give you a blank check to sin and not feel guilty about it? As long as it's socially acceptable?

And is your view of Jesus and his Father rooted in the four Gospels? It's amazing to me how many people spout off claims about Jesus that are drastically at odds with what Matthew, Mark, Luke, and John have to say. Have you *really* read them, slowly and deeply? Creating space for Jesus to fill with his reality? To allow him to define your vision of God?

Or does your view of the God whom Jesus called Father come from another source? One that's more Western, more "evolved"?

Am I hitting close to home at all?

God is not a permissive parent; neither is he an angry jerk of a dad. He's a good Father—compassionate, gracious, and slow to anger.

And remember, how you think about God, well, it will shape the way you relate to him. And the way you relate to other people. After all, *how we relate is how we relate*.[32] The way we relate to people close to us is probably a good barometer for how we relate to God. If you find yourself angry a lot, could it be that your view of God is warped by your own story? Or that you have yet to take on this aspect of God's character?

Now we're back to Exodus 34 and the imitation of God.

Yahweh is slow to anger, so *we're* to be slow to anger.

Are you?

Am I?

In all honesty, no. If you were to ask my wife or kids or close friends what my greatest flaw is, my guess is they would talk about my impatience, and my temper. I have anger issues.

I'm just learning this about myself. The last few years were a bit rocky. I hit a wall emotionally with my job. I was leading a large church with a huge staff, plus teaching and writing, all with a young family and a busy life. The stress was crippling. It started to expose cracks in my maturity, and—long story short—I burned out. Hit my limit. Went past it. Crashed.

I found myself on a three-month sabbatical, with the space to take a long, hard look at my life so far, and the once-in-a-lifetime-opportunity to reboot my story—to start over and do things differently from here on out.

So I demoted myself (which, by the way, I highly recommend), cut my hours *way back*, and made a weekly sabbath nonnegotiable. But then I went deeper. I started therapy. Holy cow, it's amazing. I had a slew of tough, but good conversations with my community. And I did a ton of reading. One of the most paradigm-shifting books for me was on emotional health.[33] Basically it was about guys like me who lead churches and honestly love Jesus, but are so emotionally out of balance that it leaks unhealth all over themselves and the people they lead.

As I was reading the chapter on family of origin, I created a little space to ask God, "What are the generational sins I carry forward? Is there anything I'm blind to? Weak points in my character I don't even see?"

Immediately, I had this sense from the Spirit that I have an anger problem.

In hindsight, this is obvious, but at the time, it was a completely virgin thought. And when I started to process this with my wife and therapist, it came out clearly: yes, I have an anger problem.

But here's why I missed it for so long: my anger isn't a yell-and-scream-and-punch-a-hole-in-the-wall kind of anger—that's why it stayed under the radar for so many years. I mean, I'm a vegetarian and a pacifist; how violent could I really be? My anger is a seething, internal kind of anger that leaks out as "constructive criticism," unkind humor, and sarcastic digs about the people closest to me. People like my wife. My kids. My community. And this sin wreaks havoc in my life. It leaves a bloody mess in its wake, crippling trust and shattering intimacy.

I see it now. I'm dealing with it. And the good news is: Jesus is changing me. Slowly, of course. I wish he would speed it up! But core tenets of personality don't change in a few months.

It takes years. But there's a trajectory I'm on—away from anger and toward mercy. I have a long way to go, but I feel like I'm en route.

Maybe for you the weak point isn't anger—it's greed or gluttony or gossip or porn or worry or illegal betting on hamster races. Whatever. We come in lots of shapes and sizes, and what's a walk in the park for one person is excruciating for the next.

But we *all* have a gap.

Between *who we are* and *who God is*.

Between the way we live and the way of Jesus.

Following Jesus is about closing that gap, one step at a time.

In closing, one of my favorite writings in the New Testament is a letter written by Jesus' brother James. He opens his letter by saying, "Everyone should be quick to listen, slow to speak, and *slow to become angry*, because human anger does not produce the righteousness that God desires."**34**

Then in chapter 5, he starts to allude to and quote from Exodus 34:

"See how the farmer waits for the land to yield its valuable crop, *patiently waiting* . . ."

"You too, be *patient* . . . because the Lord's coming is near."

"As an example of *patience* in the face of suffering, take the prophets . . ."[35]

And at the end of his section on patience in suffering, he writes, "The Lord is full of *compassion and mercy*."[36]

It's lost in translation, but that's a quote of Exodus 34v6.

Oh, and did I mention that the context for this letter is relationships? He's not writing about patience until you graduate or get the promotion or have kids or finally get to the next season of life. He's writing about people you don't get along with, don't like, and regularly get frustrated with.

Then he stacks one last command on top: "Don't grumble against one another, brothers and sisters, or you will be judged. The Judge is standing at the door!"[37]

So this whole passage is about how we treat the people who make us want to grumble. Who make us angry.

But notice his logic. For James, the "Judge is standing at the door!" Meaning, we're almost to the day when Yahweh will finally judge the earth, when every human being who ever lived will stand before their Creator, and God himself will set every wrong right. It's coming. Any day, any hour.

And because very soon Yahweh will set all the crooked things straight—*we don't have to.*

We give place to a healthy, Yahweh kind of anger over injustice, yes, and we do something about it—but we let go of our heart's warped lust for revenge.

Yahweh is the judge, not us.

Our job is simple: be like Yahweh.

Compassionate,

gracious,

and *slow to anger*.

Chapter 5

"The LORD [Yahweh], the LORD [Yahweh], the compassionate and gracious God, slow to anger, **abounding in love and faithfulness**, maintaining love to thousands, and forgiving wickedness, rebellion and sin. Yet he does not leave the guilty unpunished; he punishes the children and their children for the sin of the parents to the third and fourth generation."

Long obedience in the same direction in an age of instant gratification

Every Friday morning, my wife and I climb on our bikes and ride out to eat breakfast. Then we stop for coffee. I have Fridays off, and the kids are in school, so it's become our weekly date. The default time every week to catch up, sync our hearts, laugh, fight, make up, and talk about the things that matter.

This last Friday, we had a conversation about our upcoming anniversary: we're just about to hit fifteen years. That's a long time, right? We feel like it.

We married crazy young—she was nineteen and I was barely

twenty-one—and, honestly, it hasn't been easy. At that age, we had no clue what we were getting into. It didn't take long to figure out the obvious: we're two *very* different people, from two *very* different families of origin, with two *very* different ways of doing life. Opposites attract, true. It's the next part that's hard.[1]

So the first stretch was rough. But about seven years in, we turned a corner. I figure it takes about that long to realize you can't change your spouse to fit what my therapist calls your "ego ideal"—the picture in your mind's eye of your dream spouse perfectly cut to meet your every need and desire. My completely unscientific theory behind the "seven-year itch" is that right around year seven, you realize you have to either accept your spouse for who God made them to be, or get a divorce. We chose option A. There were no fireworks or explosions in the sky, but we started moving in a new direction. Counseling was a huge help. So was community. But mostly, we just needed time and space to relearn how to be husband and wife.

And the last few years?

Well, they've been the best by far.

So we're talking about renewing our vows for our fifteenth anniversary. Doing a little ceremony. And for us, this isn't a cute, romantic idea. Neither of us are remotely sentimental. This is a deep, meaningful, symbolic moment. We want to choose each other, *again*. And to vow—this time actually knowing what we're signing up for—to love each other "until death do us part."

After all, fifteen years is just the beginning, right?

I say all that because the next part of God's name—what makes him, *him*—is along the same lines. It's "abounding in love and faithfulness."

In Hebrew, "love and faithfulness" is *hesed* and *emet*.

Let's take each one in turn.

To start, *hesed*. This is a sweeping, panoramic word that we really have no equivalent for in English. That's why translations are all over the map. It can be translated as "steadfast love" or "unfailing love" or "covenant loyalty."

חֶסֶד .... **"Steadfast love"**
"Unfailing love"
"Covenant loyalty"

Have a look at this from the Hebrew scholar Daniel Block: "The Hebrew *hesed* cannot be translated with one English word. This is a covenant term, wrapping up in itself all the positive attributes of God."[2]

Notice that he calls *hesed* a "covenant term." Hold that in your mental dock. We'll come back to it in a few minutes.

For now, just know this is one of the most important aspects of God's character. It's the only character trait that is *repeated*. We read it here—"abounding in love and faithfulness"—and then in the next line, "maintaining love to thousands." Remember what I said about how if an ancient writer really wanted to drive a point home, he would repeat it? God speaks to his love *twice*. Back-to-back. Meaning, this is one of the truest things there is about Yahweh: he's abounding—spilling over, way past capacity—in *hesed*.

But also in *emet*, or faithfulness. Literally, the word means "truth." It's actually connected to the word "amen." Usually people say "amen" when a preacher says something that rings true deep in their bones. But *emet* can also be translated as "trustworthy." It has the idea of reliability. You can count on this God Yahweh. He won't let you down.

Unlike a lot of *us*.

When life gets hard, so many of us just bail. When it's no longer easy or fun or novel, when it gets difficult or uncomfortable or boring, we just *leave*. We leave jobs, cities, churches, friendships, marriages. We just cut ties and move on. We're a generation raised on text messaging, making flakiness easier than ever before.

God's not like that.

He's faithful.

Now, when you put *hesed* and *emet* together, it's incendiary. "Abounding in love and faithfulness" is called a hendiadys. Any lit majors out there? A hendiadys is a literary device where two nouns are smashed together to help define each other.

Meaning . . .

God's love *is* his faithfulness.

God's faithfulness *is* his love.

This is where the English translation "love" for *hesed* is incredibly deficient. As my friends would say, "It's weak sauce." When we read "love," most of us think of feelings. Or maybe tolerance. So we read "love" and think Yahweh is just saying he really likes us and feels nice, warm emotions about us.

And he does. But remember, *he's already said that*.

In English, "abounding in love" sounds like a synonym for "compassionate," so this line feels repetitive. But in Hebrew, it's not. God is saying something else here.

Hesed and *emet* are about God's loyalty—how he never, *ever* abandons his people, but he's faithful to the bitter end, no matter the cost.

This pairing of "love" and "faithfulness" is used all over the Bible. In *Psalms* alone, the word *hesed* itself is used 126 times.

For example, in Psalm 89, the poet writes:

> I will sing of the Lord's [Yahweh's] great *love* forever;
> > with my mouth I will make your *faithfulness* known
> > through all generations.
> I will declare that your *love* stands firm forever,
> > that you have established your *faithfulness* in heaven
> > itself.[3]

Then Yahweh's voice breaks into prophesy about the coming Messiah:

> "I will maintain my *love* to him forever,
> > and my covenant with him will never fail . . .
> I will not take my *love* from him,
> > nor will I ever betray my *faithfulness*."[4]

This is one sample out of *hundreds*. Not exaggerating. Yahweh's love and faithfulness are one of the major themes of the Bible, and one of the main reasons for worship in *Psalms*. It sparks poetry and music and awe and gratitude and prayer and hope.

Now, I know this raises all sorts of questions. If this is true, if God is faithful . . .

How did I end up in an unhappy marriage?

Why am I forty and still single?

How come I have a chronic illness?

Why did I have a miscarriage?

How could my best friend sleep with my fiancé?

Why was my child born with special needs?

How could I get fired from my dream job?

Why am I upside down on my mortgage?

How was I born into a world with systemic racism?

At times it's hard to reconcile God's love and faithfulness with, well, *life*.

So let's try to work this out. Together.

TWO: Stories

We can't fully wrap our heads around *hesed* and *emet* without understanding covenants. And to do that, we need at least a basic grasp on the overall story of the Bible.

Don't stress; we'll do this in a few breezy pages. Easy.

Okay, take that line I said earlier about covenants out of your mental dock. *Covenant* isn't a word we really use anymore. When I read my *New York Times* app in the morning, it doesn't report that President Trump made a "covenant" with China.

Covenant is a word from another time, another place.

In the ancient Near East, a covenant was essentially a hybrid between a promise and a legal contract. It was relational. Two (or more) people would make a promise and then sign a contract, with clearly defined blessings and curses for keeping or breaking that promise.

The closest thing we have in the modern world to a covenant is marriage. Going on fifteen years ago, when Tammy and I stared into each other's eyes on a warm June night in front of all our family and friends and said "I do," we made a covenant, a promise.

Think of the call-and-response wedding vows:

Do you so promise?

I do.

Marriage is a covenant, a promise to love and stay faithful to your spouse. But a covenant is also a binding contract. When you get married, you sign your life away. There are consequences if you don't keep your promise.

And if you know the story of the Bible, it has a lot to do with

Yahweh making covenants. And in this story—this narrative arc stretching from *Genesis* all the way to *Revelation*—there are key moments when the story leaps forward.

One of those key moments is Genesis 12. It's like the fulcrum point for the entire Old Testament. In context, Yahweh God's good, beautiful world has been defaced by evil. But then Yahweh calls a random desert Bedouin named Abram to get the story back on track.

The first thing God does with Abram is make a covenant, a promise . . .

> "I will make you into a great nation,
>> and I will bless you.
> I will make your name great,
>> and you will be a blessing.
> I will bless those who bless you,
>> and whoever curses you I will curse;
> and all peoples on earth
>> will be blessed through you."[5]

Notice all the "I will" language. That's a covenant motif. God *promises* Abram that his family will become a great nation. And he promises to bless this nation. Not just that, but he will bless "all peoples on earth" *through* this nation.

So . . .

First God will bless Abram's family.

Then, in turn, *they* will bless *the world*.

See the pattern?

God → **The** → **The**
people **world**
of God

God is saying he's going to put right everything in the world that's gone awry. All the ugly things are going to come untrue. But he's going to do this re-creative work *through* Abraham's family, later called Israel.[6]

This is a staggering promise. But please pay careful attention to its content.

God does *not* promise Abraham an easy, carefree life with money in the bank and a condo in Kauai.

God does promise to bless Abraham, but if you know the story, Abraham's life was anything but a walk in the park. The guts of the promise is that Abraham's family will function as a conduit, a medium, for Yahweh to spread his life-giving, regenerative blessing over every square inch of the earth.

And this promise later becomes a full-fledged covenant. A few chapters later, Abraham is up against a wall. It looks like Yahweh has been unfaithful to his promise. Years have passed, but Sarah is still childless, and now they're both elderly. Way past the time to, you know, make a baby.

How can a couple in AARP with infertility issues become the parents of a great nation?

Often we look at the promises of God over our lives and then compare them to our circumstances, and they just don't line up.

Enter Genesis 15. I forewarn you, it's a *weird* story that most people skip over, but it's key, so pay attention.

Yahweh tells Abraham to gather some animals and make a sacrifice—a bull, a goat, a ram, and a few birds. Abraham cuts the animals in half and spreads them out on the ground. But don't think picnic. In the ancient Near East, this was called "cutting the covenant." You would cut animals in half and lay them in a parallel line. Then the two parties would walk through the makeshift pathway of dead animals, as a symbolic way of saying, "If I don't keep my end of the promise, then may this happen to me—blood, and death."

But that's when the story takes a bizarre turn.[7] Yahweh makes Abraham fall into a deep sleep, and in it, Abraham sees a vision of God, in the image of a "smoking firepot," walking through the animals . . .

all

by

himself.

Have you ever read this story and thought to yourself, *What the heck?* If so, don't feel bad. It's kind of bizarre, but it's really a powerful moment. It's Yahweh's way of saying that even if Abraham and his children don't keep their end of the bargain, *he'll still keep his promise.* He'll rescue and save the world *through* this soon-to-be nation. No matter the cost. And if blood has to be spilled, it won't come from Abraham. It will come from Yahweh himself. He's willing to die and become like these animals just to keep his promise to bring the world back to life.

Hopefully your mind is already jumping ahead to connect the dots to Jesus. We'll get there in a second, but I want you to see that this starts millennia before the cross.

The rest of the Old Testament, really the entire Bible, is about Yahweh faithfully keeping his covenant with Abraham's family, and Israel failing miserably on her end.

When people read the Bible—especially the Old Testament—like a collection of short stories that each teach a moral lesson, it's misleading. That's *not* what it is. It's a brutally honest, raw, uncut story about God's faithfulness to Israel, and Israel's struggle to be a faithful bride in return.

What makes the Old Testament so confusing is that in the middle of all the mess—stories about murder and rape and betrayal and polygamy and domestic abuse and religious genocide and basically every horror you can think of—Yahweh is at work. He *responds*. He's involved. Coaxing good out of heinous evil. He doesn't step *back* when it gets messy; he steps *in*. He's constantly blessing—his friends, and his enemies.

One of my favorite quotes of Exodus 34 in the Old Testament is in a memoir from a politician named Nehemiah. He writes at a low point in Israel's story. She's in exile in Babylon. He and a small band of Hebrews are back in Jerusalem, trying to rebuild the walls, but it's not going all that well.

And in a famous prayer, he says this: "You are a *forgiving* God, *gracious* and *compassionate*, *slow to anger* and *abounding in love*. Therefore you did not desert them."[8]

Hopefully by now you can pick out all the language from Exodus 34. Nehemiah, like any good Hebrew, is steeped in the name of God.

Then he says *this*: "Now therefore, our God, the great God, mighty and awesome, who *keeps his covenant of love*, do not let all this hardship seem trifling in your eyes . . . In all that has happened to us, you have remained righteous; you have acted *faithfully*, while we acted wickedly."[9]

For Nehemiah, even the *exile* was a sign of Yahweh's faithfulness. He hadn't abandoned Israel, even if it felt that way. Like a good father, he let Israel go into exile to discipline her. But Nehemiah sees a day coming when Yahweh will keep his promise, and he begs for that day to come.

And what does Nehemiah pray for? The God who "keeps his covenant of love" (*hesed*) and is "faithful" (*emet*).

But he never gets to see the answer to his prayer—not fully. For that, you have to wait for Jesus . . .

THREE: Jesus

For two millennia, theologians have been wrestling with the mystery that is Jesus of Nazareth. In Jesus, divinity and humanity coexist. God and man overlap and join together.

Jesus is Yahweh in flesh and blood.

But here's what you need to see: he's also *Israel* in flesh and blood. He's Israel's king, her representative, drawing her story onto his shoulders.

He's Yahweh,

and he's Israel,

in the same place.

We've already made the point (way back in chapter 1) that the writer John's famous line about how Jesus was "full of grace and truth" is actually a quote from Exodus 34. It's lost in the translation from Hebrew to Greek and then to English (yup, that's confusing), but John is saying that Jesus is the embodiment of *hesed* and *emet*.

Jesus came to do what Abraham and Israel were supposed to do, but never could. He came to bless the world.

All because thousands of years ago, Yahweh made a promise. When Israel failed, Yahweh was faithful. Even before that, when *Adam* failed, he was faithful. And when *you and I* failed, God was still faithful. To bless and heal and free and save.

Jesus takes all our failure—millennia of broken promises—and he drags it to the cross, absorbing it in his death and then breaking its hold over humanity through his resurrection.

This is why the writers of the New Testament are constantly quoting from the Old.[10] For them, the gospel started in Genesis 12, not Matthew 1.[11] Yahweh made a promise, and he was faithful to the point of death. *And he's still not done!* He will keep *all* of his promises. Jesus will return and see to it.

And it's because of Yahweh's love and faithfulness that we can look forward to a world set free from the entropy of death.

We can hope for this, plan on it, bank on it.

Now, when I say "hope," I don't mean wishful thinking,

"I hope I get a parking place quickly."

"I hope the next *Star Wars* movie is good." Please, Jesus . . .

"I hope she texts me back."

"I hope I get a tax refund."

Good luck with *that*.

To the Scripture writers, **hope is the absolute expectation of coming good based on the character of God**.

It's bedrock trust that no matter how many wrong turns we make or setbacks we face, we can sleep soundly tonight because we know that, one day, Yahweh will eradicate evil forever. He will remake the world into a garden city, a second Eden. He will bless "all peoples on earth" through his Son, Jesus.

And it's all because Yahweh is "abounding in love and faithfulness."

FOUR: Us

Now, thank you for your patience. Or should I say, *faithfulness*. I tell you all these stories from the Old Testament for this reason:

Israel's story is *your* story.

Like our spiritual parents, we've failed, over and over again, but God has been faithful.

I love how Paul puts it in his letter to Timothy: "If we are faithless, he remains faithful, for he cannot disown himself."[12]

Paul is right to see that Yahweh's faithfulness is intrinsic to his name, his nature. He could no sooner be unfaithful than he could lie or cheat or steal.

And God is faithful, *even when we're not*. Even when we're flaky and skittish and drop the ball.

But there are times when it doesn't feel that way. When it feels like God is anything but faithful. When your wife is ninety and *still* not pregnant and you think, *God, where are you?*

Now I think we're finally ready to deal with the "yeah, but" questions we all have . . .

My dad died when I was ten. How is God faithful?

I just went through a nasty divorce, and now I'm left alone with two kids and an alimony check that doesn't even cover rent. How is God faithful?

I was just diagnosed with spinal meningitis, and I'm in and out of the hospital monthly. If God is faithful, why am I in so much pain?

Well, remember the covenant! What did God promise? An easy life? Health and wealth? No. To bless the world through his people.

When we say that God is faithful, we don't mean you'll never experience suffering. A lot of people—in particular, Americans—misinterpret God's faithfulness to mean some kind of promise to give us life, liberty, and the pursuit of happiness. So when tragedy strikes or the economy goes south or the child tests positive or we don't find a spouse by thirty, we think God is *unfaithful*.

But that's a gross misreading of God's promise to Abraham. God never said we would live trouble-free. Honestly, Jesus made the *opposite* promise: "In this world you will have trouble. But take heart! I have overcome the world."[13] This is one of the many promises in the Bible we tend to skip over and ignore.

It's not that God doesn't want you to live a rich and satisfying life—I believe he does. He's your Father. What father doesn't want success and prosperity for his kids? But like any good father, he takes the long view. He's willing to discipline his kids to see them grow and mature into their full potential.

God is more concerned with your long-term character than your short-term happiness. And he's more than willing to sacrifice the one to get to the other.

Plus, God doesn't always get what he wants. Not yet. Remember Jesus' prayer: "your will be done."[14] There are other wills at play on earth, many of them at odds with God's heart for your life.

As I see it, God does *use* evil, but he's not responsible for evil, ever. Things like cancer or HIV/AIDS or abuse or, obviously, our own mistakes—this stuff doesn't come from God. Evil is a cruel, alien intruder into God's good world. His enemy, not his friend.

But tragically, many people don't see it that way. As I said before, this is an area of disagreement in the church. And I respect the mystery of evil. There's a curtain to the universe that most of us never get to see behind. Three very important words we all need to say regularly are, "*I don't know.*" But still, I deeply believe a lot of people are angry with God for stuff he had nothing to do with.

Blaming God for the death of a loved one or the failure of your business is like my son Moses coming home from school mad at me because he got a bad grade on his test or fell at recess and hurt his leg.

What?

God quickly becomes a scapegoat for the immature or confused.

So many people are hyperfatalistic in how they think about life, constantly dropping the cliché "God's in control." But is he? Of *everything*? Even *evil*? Are you sure about that?

It seems to me that the story the Scripture writers tell is far more complex. God's will is one will among many, and he's patiently sorting through the messes of our lives, giving ample space for our free will and decisions, but graciously drawing good out of evil. As one New Testament writer put it, "In all things God works for the good of those who love him."[15]

If this sounds *less* hopeful to you, it's not. Think about it. This means that even when lousy stuff happens to us that is clearly against the will of God—we come down with a life-threatening disease; we bury a close friend; we fail at a marriage, etc.—even *then,* God is far more powerful than any evil we face. And he has the judo-like ability to turn evil on its head and somehow co-opt it for good.

Our hope isn't that nothing bad will ever happen to us.

Or that everything that does happen to us is "the will of God."

Our hope is that no matter what happens to us, *Jesus is back from the dead*, and anything is possible.

Yes, sometimes things go horribly wrong. But the resurrection is a megaphone turned up to 11, screaming, *God is bigger than evil! And stronger than death!* The empty tomb dwarfs every tragedy we ever face with his promise to make all things beautiful in their time.

What I'm getting at is this: God's promise isn't that you'll marry your dream spouse, get famous, make a ton of money, and retire at forty on a golf course in California.

God's promise is that he will *bless* you, so you can turn around and do the same for others. He'll put you to rights, so you can you put the world to rights. And one day, in time, he'll return to finish what he started and set all the crooked things straight.

And God's promises aren't just generic to all his followers; they are specific to you.

One of the greatest mistakes people make, especially our friends in the prosperity gospel tradition, is claiming promises that God made to other people as their own. For example, taking a promise from Isaiah—that God will "enlarge the place of your tent . . . For you will spread out to the right and the left; your descendants will dispossess nations and settle in their desolate cities"[16]—and allegorizing it into a promise about how God will give you money for your home addition or a new campus for your megachurch. I cringe when I hear people abuse the Bible to bolster a twisted version of the American Dream.

Or—here's another example—when people take a *principle* in the Bible and turn it into a *promise*. For example, taking a line out of *Proverbs* like, "Train up a child in the way he should go: and when he is old he will not depart from it,"[17] and claiming it as a promise for your wayward teenager.

But that aside, there is some truth to the idea of God making promises to *you*, individually. I believe there are sacred moments when the Spirit of God whispers to our spirit a promise, a vision of what *will* be, in his time.

Like Abraham and Sarah, these whispers often come years before they turn into Isaacs. And they often seem unlikely, if not impossible. The waiting can push your faith to the limit. There will be many days when it seems like everything in your present contradicts God's promise over your future.

What has God promised you? When you get quiet before God, what rumbles deep down in your soul? What longing, what ache, what sense of destiny that you just can't shake?

God will be faithful to his promise. No matter what. No matter how many times you trip over your feet, no matter what other "wills" get in the way, God is greater. And he's loving, and faithful.

This is what God is like.

Now, before we close the door on this chapter, let's flip it around— from God to us. Let's not forget: we are Yahweh's people, his bride. Our role in the relationship is to mirror and mimic our husband's character to the world.

Are we faithful?

Are you?

Am I?

As a generation, the idea of faithfulness is alien and strange. Our grandparents knew a thing or two about it, but not us.

The average stay in a marriage is about eight years;[18] my grandparents were married for sixty.

The average stay in a job is four years, and every year it drops;[19] my grandfather worked as a nuclear engineer for GE for thirty-five years. Who does that anymore?

Faithfulness has become like disco—it used to be cool, and a few people still do it, but for the most part, it's a thing of the past.

And here's the problem with that: the best things in life are the result of faithfulness. Usually years, if not decades, of faithfulness.

Faithfulness is long obedience in the same direction in an age of instant gratification.[20]

I want a shortcut to life—I was raised on the microwave and VISA and Amazon Prime and instant messaging and TV on Demand. The world at my fingertips. I want it all, and I want it all *right now*. But there are no shortcuts to life. You can't microwave character. It's more like a tree that you grow slowly, one season after another. There are summer-like seasons were you can pluck joy off the limbs, where your life is dripping with growth and abundance. And there are winter-like seasons, where life feels slow and empty. The best trees are the ones that stay rooted and just keep at it.

So I want to be faithful in summer and winter. To stay the course, no matter how hard it gets.

After all, that's what God is like.

Think about the implications this has for marriage. Maybe your marriage is difficult. Mine was, for years. And there are seasons when Tammy and I revert back to old, unhealthy ways. What would it look like for you to stay faithful to the vows you made, through all the emotional highs and lows of life together?

Or think about your career. It might be smart to jump to a new job every few years, depending on your field, but to master your craft and become incredibly good at whatever it is you do—parenting or architecture or teaching or business management or flying airplanes—takes decades. You can't do what you love until you're good at what you do. But sociologists argue that to become really good at your craft takes most people about ten thousand hours—that's at least a decade of hard work. What would it look like to seize upon a dream for your life and run after it? Not at a sprint, but at a slow, steady pace, ready to wait for a very long time to see God's calling on your life materialize and bloom to life?

Or think about your city and your place in it—church and neighborhood and relationships. We're so rootless. So transient. More tourist than citizen. But what would it look like for you to be faithful to the kingdom of God in your place, not for a few months or years, but for a lifetime?

The question I want to leave you with is this: Where has God called you to be faithful?

Stop and think about it for a minute.

No, really. Stop and think about it.

What comes to mind?

Whatever it is, the odds are that it will be hard work. It will be painfully slow. And frustrating at times. The best things in life always are. But trust me, *it will be worth it*.

So keep at it, my friends. Don't give up. Not yet. Be faithful, like the God you worship.

And never forget to live in the moment, because the moment is all we have.

Chapter 6

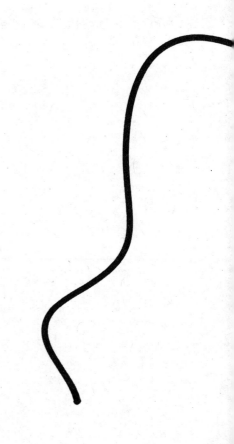

"The LORD [Yahweh], the LORD [Yahweh], the compassionate and gracious God, slow to anger, abounding in love and faithfulness, **maintaining love to thousands, and forgiving wickedness, rebellion and sin. Yet he does not leave the guilty unpunished; he punishes the children and their children for the sin of the parents to the third and fourth generation.**"

The God who just won't stop until you're completely free

I know what you're thinking.

The question in the back of your mind. The pit in your stomach, all that anxiety building, churning, amping up with each turn of the page . . .

What in the world is up with the *end*? The closing line about how Yahweh "punishes the children and their children for the sin of the parents"—what's up with *that*?

How can Yahweh be "compassionate and gracious" and "slow to anger" and "abounding in love and faithfulness" if he goes MMA *on kids*?

I've been looking forward to this.

There are two types of people in the world: bad-news-first people, and slackers. I'm not a slacker. So let's start off with the bad news.

Here it is: we don't get to pick and choose with the Scriptures. As followers of Jesus, we follow our Rabbi's example. He took the Scriptures *very* seriously.[1] So do we. We come under the authority of Scripture as an expression of our submission to Jesus as Lord. *All* of Scripture. We don't skim the Bible and pull out the parts we like and then eject anything that doesn't fit with our late-modern, Western, progressive views. When we get to something we don't like, we *deal* with it. We question and probe and study and nuance and wrestle and maybe even protest it, but in the end, hopefully, we say yes to it. Even if the pill is hard to swallow.

Maybe you read the Bible differently. That's fine. But I think you would agree that if you shape your theology of God from *bits* and *pieces* of the Bible, along with a mishmash of your own bias, pop culture, and the ever-evolving (or maybe just *changing*?) tide of ethics in Western culture, then you'll end up with a "God" who is simply a projection of your own wishful thinking. A God who isn't real, but artificial, made to order in a laboratory, not grown in the soil of reality.

The nice thing about made-up gods is they agree with you on everything and let you live as you please. Unfortunately, they are incredibly boring and flat and humdrum—because they don't actually exist.

Then there's the even more terrifying possibility that you'll end up with a "god" who *is* real, but isn't the one true Creator God, and who plays to your I-want-it-all-now desires, only to turn on you once you're hooked in.

Yahweh might not look exactly how we want him to look, at least not at first. But as we begin to see his character, as his beauty starts to come into focus, we realize that who he is, is so much better than who we wanted him to be.

So that's the bad news.

The good news is this: I can confidently say, this aspect of God that we are about to unpack is, well, good. It's beautiful. And it rings true.

So let's get into it. We have a fair bit of ground to cover in this chapter because we have an entire sentence to work through, not just a few words. So we'll work through it line by line and get to the part about Yahweh punishing kids near the end.

That should keep you reading . . .

To start off, the opening line *of the closing line* is

"maintaining love to thousands . . ."

Once again, we hear of Yahweh's *hesed*, or covenant love, but this time we read that he's "maintaining" it. The root word here is *ntsr*, which means "to protect" or "to guard."

This language is reused by the psalmist:

> Do not withhold your *mercy* from me, LORD [Yahweh];
> may your love and faithfulness always protect me.[2]

By now, all the Exodus language should pop out to you—mercy, love, faithfulness. The poet is praying for Yahweh's character to *ntsr* him, to watch over him and keep him from evil, specifically evil people.

Yahweh is like a sentry on guard. He wants to make *sure* that you get his *hesed*. But not just you! He's "maintaining love *to thousands*." The idea here is the scope of Yahweh's *hesed*. It's not just for a few of his favorites—it's *limitless*. There's no ceiling, no bottom.

Next, Yahweh says that he is

"forgiving wickedness, rebellion and sin . . ."

A lot of people think of forgiveness as something Jesus introduced. As if it was a new concept, foreign to Moses and the writers of the Old Testament. But that just shows how little time we spend in the Bible. The English word *forgive* is used all through the Hebrew Scriptures.

In Exodus 34v7, the Hebrew word translated as "forgiving" is *nasa*, and it literally means "to lift up," "to carry," or "to take away."

Talk about a signpost pointing forward to Jesus. Not to get ahead of myself, but that's exactly what he does on the cross. He lifts sin onto his shoulders and then takes it away—straight into the maw of hell itself. John the Baptizer called Jesus "the Lamb of God, who *takes away* the sin of the world!"[3]

What does Yahweh forgive? Well, the language here is "wicked-ness, rebellion and sin"—the three most common words in the Hebrew Bible for the extent of human depravity.

"Wickedness" is *avon* in Hebrew. It's a junk-drawer word that basically means any kind of bad behavior—everything from cutting off an elderly driver in traffic to genocide.

"Rebellion" is the word *pesha*. It means "to break the law." *Pesha* is a legal word, the type used in a courtroom. It's a crime. A viola-tion. It's when we know exactly what God commands, and we say, "I'll do as I please, thank you very much."

And "sin" is *hata*, which means "to miss the mark." It's a word picture: visualize an archer and a target. He pulls the bow back and lets it fly. To "sin" is to miss the bull's-eye. It wasn't actually a moral word in Moses' time. It just meant to mess up.

Now, these three words join together to cover the full breadth of human pollution. But the point here isn't to lay on a guilt trip; it's that *Yahweh is forgiving of sins of all shapes and sizes*.

Notice, it's not just that he forgives.

It's that he is forgiving.

You see that?

In a poetic allusion to Exodus 34, the prophet Micah speaks to the forgiving nature of Yahweh:

> Who is a God like you,
>> who pardons *sin* and forgives the *transgression*
>> of the remnant of his inheritance?
>
> You do not stay *angry* forever
>> but delight to show *mercy*.
>
> You will again have *compassion* on us;
>> you will tread our *sins* underfoot
>> and hurl all our *iniquities* into the depths of the sea.[4]

So forgiveness grows out of God's *name*, his character. It flows from Yahweh's inner essence, the deepest, truest parts of his being. As one heavyweight scholar said in his commentary on Exodus 34, "He does not reluctantly forgive sins against himself and others; he does so eagerly, as a manifestation of his character."[5]

What a great line: "he does so eagerly."

It's like Yahweh is *itching* to forgive. Like he's up early every morning, thinking, *Who can I forgive today?*

It's who he *is*.

But there's a counterpoint to the forgiving nature of God:

"Yet he does not leave the guilty unpunished . . ."

This is a slippery phrase to translate into English. Another translation gets us a little closer to the original Hebrew: "but who will by
no means *clear the guilty*."[6] The idea here is that Yahweh is forgiving by nature, but at the same time, he's also *just*. He doesn't let
the guilty off the hook.

There are lots of people who don't *want* forgiveness.

Some because they deny they are sinful. After all, the Western,
secular worldview we grew up with essentially denies human
sinfulness. The idea that "all have sinned and fall short of the glory
of God,"[7] that each of us is born bent, that something deep in
the core of our being is warped out of shape—this is out of step
with our time, a hangover from a religious, traditional world we
want desperately to move on from, and a kind of cultural heresy
in our new post-Christian world. The Western world's blind faith
in politics, education, and the next "killer app" to usher in our
own godless utopia is hopelessly naive, at best. And because our
society denies that "all have sinned," it's forced to blame somebody *else* for the evils of the world. Listen to talk radio for five
minutes—it's nonstop blame shifting. The right blames the ACLU,
illegal immigrants, and Muslims; the left, religion, unsophisticated
"folk" from small towns and rural communities, and hedge fund
managers. Whatever the issue—the economy, terrorism, health
care—it's always somebody else's fault. This ongoing denial is
deeply fracturing to our society and, even more so, to our relationship with God. If we refuse to even admit we are sinful, then we

can't receive Yahweh's forgiveness. Forgiveness is like a gift—you have to reach out, take it, and open the box; you have to say yes to it.

Others are well aware of how screwed up we human beings are; they just don't care. They don't deny human sinfulness; if anything, they brag about it. Unapologetic and unrepentant, they keep on in sin, no matter the collateral damage to others or trauma to God's heart.

Yahweh doesn't turn a blind eye to either camp. He doesn't wink at sin. *Oh well! Boys will be boys!*

Never.

He's just.

And Yahweh's justice is a *good* thing. I cringe when I read, "He does not leave the guilty unpunished." Even when I nuance it out, it's still terrifying. But remember, God's end goal is a world with *no* evil. Yahweh's justice isn't about retribution or payback or some kind of God-size vendetta—it's about the healing and renewal of the world. That's why it's not rigid; it's flexible. It has a bend and pliability to it. He's highly sensitive to any change of direction. When we repent, he's *responds*. With mercy. But if we don't repent, then he'll only wait for so long before he puts a stop to our rampage.

Because evil is the by-product of sin, and Yahweh is after a world with no evil. No garment workers in Bangladesh slaving twelve hours a day, seven days a week, in dangerous conditions for barely enough money to survive, all so we can buy a T-shirt for five bucks. No cruel dictators driving an economy into the ground with war, "ethnic cleansing," and rampant corruption. No abuse, no shootings in elementary schools, no violence at all. No racism, no misogyny, no exploitation of women and children. No anxiety, no depression, no mental illness. No divorce, no betrayal, no break-down of the family, no fatherless children—*no evil at all*.

How many of you want to live in that kind of a world?

You can.

If you're a follower of Jesus, one day *you will*.

Because Yahweh is just.

And this is a *good* thing! It's part of the good news. The hope of the gospel isn't that Holocaust survivors will stand next to Hitler for eternity or that a victim of domestic abuse will live forever with her husband. The hope is that there will be *no* Hitlers, no women thrown across the room in anger, no slave traders, no genocidal maniacs, no suicide bombers storming into crowded markets, no Predator drones flying over your house as your five-year-old cow-ers in fear—nothing and nobody who is openly hostile to the way of Jesus, *because God will put an end to evil once and for all*.

The judge will *finally* judge.

And we want justice.

We crave it.

We ache for it, deep in our bones.

Every time we see another story about a Ponzi scheme on Wall Street or a violent uprising in Africa or racist violence here in the U.S.—every time we see evil—we have this acute, gut-level pain. We think, *Will somebody* please *do something about this?*

As the prophet Amos said, "Let justice roll on like a river."[8]

One day, it will. Right now, Yahweh's justice is a trickle. But one day it will turn into a river, and from there into an ocean blanketing the world. When Jesus comes again, he will cripple sin for good and bring evil to its knees forever.

So, to put it all together . . .

Because Yahweh is forgiving, we don't have to cower in fear and dread Jesus' return. We can take our "wickedness, rebellion and sin" straight to the cross and let it die on Jesus' shoulders.

And because Yahweh is also just, we can look forward to a day when his Son, Jesus, will judge the world, banish evil forever, and lead humanity to a glorious horizon.

That's the gospel.

Unfortunately, you're still thinking, *Yes, great, but what about how Yahweh punishes kids?*

That's the next, unsettling line:

"he punishes the children and their children for the sin of the parents . . ."

What could this possibly mean?

Well, for starters, it can't mean what it sounds like at face value. At least not in my English translation—that Yahweh punishes kids for their parents' sin.

Here's why: Moses later makes the exact *opposite* point: "Parents are not to be put to death for their children, nor children put to death for their parents; *each will die for their own sin.*"[9]

Is Moses contradicting himself?

Or listen to the prophet Jeremiah's commentary on this tricky line from Exodus 34: "You show love to thousands but bring the punishment for the parents' sins into the laps of their children after them . . . *you reward each person according to their conduct and as their deeds deserve.*"[10]

Hmmm . . .

So if Yahweh is *not* saying that if Grandma cheats on her taxes, he will take it out on little Jonny, what *is* he saying?

Well, there are layers of meaning to the text. Track with me . . .

The first layer is that the parents' sin has consequences for the children's future. This is the obvious, axiomatic meaning. And we all know it's true.

If Dad and Mom run a meth lab and are arrested by the police and land in jail, it's the children who will suffer the most. They'll end up in the foster care system. Without the family God intended. Often passed from home to home, with no stability. If they don't get placed into a good family, they could easily end up dumped out on the street at eighteen. But even if they land in a healthy, Jesus-following family, like the many in my church that do foster care, they will still enter adulthood with the handicap of their parents' mistakes.

Or to bring it closer to home: if Dad and Mom get a divorce, the children will suffer the fallout. In spite of our culture's ridiculous PR campaign to sell divorce as a danger-free zone for kids, we all know it's a sham. The mop-up from a marriage gone awry is incalculable—grief, trust issues, insecurity, economic strain, messy holidays, the fear of commitment later in life. When parents sin, the children are collateral damage.

But that's not all Yahweh is saying. **The next layer of meaning is that sin runs in the family.** Sin, like your DNA, like the color of your eyes or your physique or your "quirky" personality, is passed down from one generation to the next.

One generation's sin often becomes the next generation's sin,

and the next,

and the *next*.

My sister—Betes!—just had a baby. Birdie James. Now, I want to think of my beautiful infant niece as innocent—a blank canvas. But she's not. None of us are. We all come into the world carrying truckloads of baggage from our family line. Even today—in what is hands down the most individualistic society *ever*—we have sayings like "like father, like son" or "the apple doesn't fall far from the tree."

We vow, "I will never be like my father or mother or grandfather or that weird aunt on my mother's side." But then, to our dismay, we see the exact same dysfunctional patterns resurface in our own life.

Some of us just can't escape our last name.

All of which leads me to the last layer, where we hit bedrock. I would argue, it's the main idea: **because Yahweh is just, he will continue to punish sin in each and every generation until it's completely gone.**

Put another way, don't think that because God punished your daddy for idolatry, you're off the hook for your own idolatry. God will punish you, the same way he punished your father. The same way he punished your grandfather. The same way he punished your great-grandfather. Because his end goal is a world free from evil, and he won't stop until the eradication of sin in your family line is complete.

If this is unnerving for you, keep reading. The last phrase is my favorite part:

"to the third and fourth generation."

The ending is a twist, a surprise. And it's incredibly cool.

The word *generation* isn't there in Hebrew. It was added for English readers to make sense of an awkward Hebrew idiom. Scholars point out that Exodus 34v6–7 has a poetic rhythm to it,[11] and whatever word comes after "thousands" may also come after "to the third and fourth." So it could read:

"maintaining love to thousands *of generations* . . .

and

he punishes the children to the third and fourth *generation*."

But more literally, we could translate it:

"maintaining love to thousands . . .

and

he punishes the children to the third and fourth."

You see the picture?

Imagine a scale in your mind's eye. Not the one in your bathroom that makes you feel guilty for the pizza you ate last night. The one in Washington, D.C., of Lady Justice, with a fulcrum point in the middle and a weight on either side.

Now imagine it uneven.

On one side is Yahweh's mercy.

On the other is God's justice.

But they are way out of balance. The imagery here is of a scale that's weighted to the side of mercy. He punishes to the third and fourth, yes, but he's "maintaining love to *thousands*."

As one New Testament writer later put it, "Mercy triumphs over judgment."[12]

Yahweh is just. And that's good news. That's why we can look forward to a better tomorrow. But he's also forgiving. He can't help but show mercy; it's who he is. And when his justice and mercy bump up against each other—when they conflict and bang heads and square off—*mercy wins every time*.

TWO: Stories

We see this tension in Yahweh's character—this inner tug-of-war between his mercy and justice—play out all over the Scriptures.

I want to take you to a story in Numbers 14. It's one of the few stories where the second half of Exodus 34v6–7 is quoted. Usually Scripture writers just quote the first part—about how Yahweh is compassionate and gracious and slow to anger. That makes sense. We tend to focus on the aspects of God we like and push to the side the parts we don't. But in Numbers 14, there's a quote of the thorny line at the end.

Here's the context: Israel is in a bad way. They've finally come to the edge of Canaan—this new, exotic home they've been traveling to for over a year. As you would say in 1500 BC—"a land flowing with milk and honey."[13] But when they arrive, they learn the land is filled with Amalekites—a barbaric, masochistic tribe of ancient warriors. And they have *giants*. In a world of hand-to-hand combat, giants are like nukes.

What chance do a band of peasant ex-slaves have against *that*?

So the people rebel. They refuse to cross the Jordan River. "We should choose a leader and go back to Egypt," they say.[14]

Moses and his brother, Aaron, do their best to talk Israel down. But it's no good: "The whole assembly talked about stoning them."[15]

The problem is the people don't trust Yahweh. They don't really believe he's compassionate and gracious, a parent-like God caring for his kids. So they sin.

Sin, at its root, is not trusting God.

We want to make it about temptation and a lack of self-control, and it is. But really, under the facade, it's about not trusting Yahweh's character.

Think back to Adam and Eve in the Garden. Yahweh puts two trees in the middle of Eden. One is the "tree of life"—if they eat from that tree, they will live forever. The other is the "tree of the knowledge of good and evil," but it's off-limits. If they eat from that tree, God says, "You will certainly die."[16]

One tree, life.

The other, death.

Pretty straightforward, right?

But what does the snake say to Eve?

"You will not certainly die . . . For God knows that when you eat from it your eyes will be opened, and you will be like God."[17]

You see what he's doing? How subtle and smart he is? He's implying that she can't trust God. That God has ulterior motives, an agenda. He doesn't have her good in mind.

So Eve has a decision to make: trust God. Have faith that he wants the best for her. *Or* trust the snake, and her own judgment. Go with her feelings.

And who does Eve trust?

Exactly.

Now, if you're new to the Bible, a story about a talking snake and a naked woman speaking Parseltongue in front of a magic tree sounds ridiculous. I feel ya.

Are we reading narrative here? Poetry? Parable?[18]

Honestly, that's beside the point.

The point is: *from the beginning of the story*, human beings are lousy at trusting God. Eve's blood is in our DNA. We've *all* been there, fruit in hand, the serpent's voice in our ear. We've all made the wrong choice. Simply because we don't trust in God's name.

That's exactly what we see play out in Numbers 14. The people don't trust Yahweh. And so they sin—they openly rebel and dig their heels in on the wrong side of the Jordan.

And what happens? It's not good.

Yahweh says to Moses, "How long will these people treat me with contempt? How long will they refuse to believe in me, in spite of all the signs I have performed among them? I will strike them down with a plague and destroy them, but I will make you into a nation greater and stronger than they."[19]

Yahweh essentially says he's going to start over with Moses. Now, you would think Moses would say, *Fantastic!* Israel is a pain in the neck. Nothing but trouble for the prophet. But Moses is starting to take on the character of his God. He says to Yahweh, "Then the Egyptians will hear about it!'"[20]

He's haggling with God—telling him to think about his *name*, his reputation, what the other nations will think of him.

Then he quotes Exodus 34v6–7 *back to Yahweh*.

"Now may the Lord's strength be displayed, just as you have declared: 'The LORD [Yahweh] is *slow to anger, abounding in love and forgiving sin and rebellion. Yet he does not leave the guilty unpunished; he punishes the children for the sins of the parents to the third and fourth generation*.' In accordance with your great love, forgive the sin of these people, just as you have pardoned them from the time they left Egypt until now."[21]

Again: Moses is calling Yahweh *to be Yahweh*. To be true to his character.

To be forgiving.

And Yahweh *immediately* says, "I have forgiven them, as you asked."

When it comes to mercy, you don't have to twist God's arm.

If this story feels like déjà vu, it's for good reason. This is the *second* time Yahweh was going to destroy Israel, and the *second* time Moses talked God out of it, and the *second* time God *naha-me*d, or changed his mind.

And you know what they say about when God repeats himself . . .

I love stories like this because they blow up the image of a cold, robotic God up in the sky who runs the universe like an automated machine, like the future is a pre-mapped journey. Instead, Yahweh is a *person*. He's God, swimming in mystery we will never understand, but somehow, when we pray, he listens and—you ready to say it again?—*responds*! He's interactive and malleable and open to suggestions.

But I've already made that point. A dozen times. Because if you really want to drive a point home, you . . .

Okay, I'll stop now.

This story still isn't over. The next line is haunting.

"Nevertheless, as surely as I live . . . not one of them will ever see the land I promised on oath to their ancestors . . . As for your children that you said would be taken as plunder, I will bring them in to enjoy the land you have rejected. But as for you, your bodies

will fall in this wilderness. Your children will be shepherds here for forty years, suffering for your unfaithfulness."[22]

Man, that is a huge killjoy: "nevertheless."

Yahweh was forgiving. They were still his people. Mercy came out on top. But an entire generation ended up dying in the wilderness.

Nevertheless . . .

They simply were not the kind of people who could step into the land. God had to wait for a new generation to come up in the ranks, and try again.

And notice the case in point: the children suffer for the parents' sin! Wandering behind Mom and Dad in the desert.

The point of this story is this: **Yahweh is forgiving, *but sin is not*.**

Sin is *un*forgiving—merciless, petty, and cruel.

Our sin has consequences. We can miss out on blessing irretrievably. We can end up like Israel—forgiven, yes, but lost in the trackless desert waste.

To borrow from my overused analogy, let's say I were to have an affair, cheat on my wife, betray my family, profane the very nature of trust itself. But then let's say I were to repent, break it off, and go crawling back to my family and my God. I have no doubt that God would forgive me.

But I would spend the rest of my life picking up the pieces.

At best, my marriage would suffer a catastrophic breach of trust; at worst, it could easily come to a swift and terrible end. It would take me years to re-earn my children's respect, if ever. I'm a pastor, so I would immediately lose my job. Between my lack of marketable skills and my duty to pay alimony, I would quickly devolve into poverty. I'm sure my community would come around me, but my reputation would now carry a stigma with it. It would take me decades to rebuild a cheap copy of the life I once had.

Yeah, I'm not planning on *ever* cheating on my wife.

But then again, who does?

What I'm saying is that we need to take sin *way. more. seriously.*

If your heart is heavy and you feel sick to your stomach right now, good—that's the healthy, emotionally mature response to the gravity of sin.

Does God forgive? Constantly. Does he wipe the slate clean and help people start over? All the time. Is there healing in Jesus? Yes.

But we still need to grapple with the weight of sin, because we don't want to miss out on blessing! We don't want to stare over the waters of Jordan, right on the cusp of the life God has for us, only to throw it all away and spend years of our life in regret.

THREE: Jesus

So there's a tension here between mercy and justice—a tension that goes back a very long time. You feel it on every page of the Bible. As the story goes on, you start to think, *How is God going to resolve this?*

And the resolution finally comes, not in a brilliant lecture by a well-known theologian, but in a rabbi from Nazareth named Jesus.

Remember the Exodus 34 allusion from John's gospel about how "the Word became flesh and made his dwelling among us"?[23] Well, John goes on to say that Jesus is "the Lamb of God, who takes away the sin of the world."[24]

Lamb of God?

Sheep of Yahweh?

This is tapping into the rich, ancient Hebrew tradition of animal sacrifice. For more than a thousand years, the way Yahweh would deal with sin was through blood.[25] If you screwed up (or maybe better to say, *when* you screwed up), you would go to the temple in Jerusalem, and you would bring an animal with you—usually a lamb. You would place your hand on the animal's head, and the priest would slit its throat and burn its carcass on the altar. The lamb would suffer and die *in your place*.

You sin. The lamb dies.

The lamb dies. You live on in God's favor.

As gory and premodern and non-vegan as this sounds, the whole thing was a signpost pointing forward to Jesus. It's clear, all throughout the Old Testament, that the entire sacrificial system is temporary. It's a stopgap until Yahweh comes up with a better way to reconcile his mercy and justice.

In the meantime, it's brilliant. Yahweh was introducing his people to what theologians call "substitutionary atonement"—the idea that someone else can die in your place. Someone else can take the punishment for your crime. This was a revolutionary new idea at the time.

For a millennium, that "someone else" was a lamb.

Until Jesus. The "Lamb of God."[26]

One of the most stunning reflections on the meaning of Jesus' death is found in *Romans*. It's chock-full of language about how Jesus is the sacrifice to end all sacrifices. How he died in *our* place.

Paul writes, "God presented Christ as a *sacrifice* of atonement, through the shedding of his blood—to be received by faith. He did this to demonstrate his righteousness, because in his forbearance he had left the sins committed beforehand *unpunished*—he did it to demonstrate his righteousness at the present time, so as to be just and the one who justifies those who have faith in Jesus."[27]

With a clever play on words, Paul is saying that Jesus' death is the solution to the ancient dilemma of God's mercy and justice.[28] The cross is an expression of Yahweh's mercy—it's his way of "forgiving wickedness, rebellion and sin." But it's also an expression of God's justice—"he does not leave the guilty unpunished."

He's just . . .

and he's the justifier.

In this moment we see—more clearly than ever before—what Yahweh is like. The reconciliation of God's mercy and justice in the death of Jesus is the ultimate expression of God's character. The tension is finally resolved. It's in God's nature to show mercy and forgive, but it's also in his nature to deal with sin, and these two parts of God's person—seemingly at odds for so many years—finally come together on the cross in beautiful harmony.

Open your eyes: *This is what God is like.*

In spite of all the talk in the Bible about Yahweh's wrath, nobody should ever accuse Yahweh of being mean. Yes, he gets angry, but he takes that anger *on himself.* He doesn't make you and me pay for our sin—*he* pays for it. With the currency of his own blood.

We sin. Jesus dies.

Jesus dies. We live on in relationship with the Father.

Welcome to the kingdom of God, my friends.

Think of how categorically different this is from all the other "gods." Remember Artemis and King Agamemnon? The goddess was so angry that she made the king sacrifice his own daughter.

But *this* God—the one true Creator God—he doesn't demand we give up our children for human sacrifice. Instead, *he* gives up *his* Son.

And Jesus isn't acting on his own; it's the Father and the Son working together. For all my life, I've heard preachers say, "The Father poured out his wrath on the Son." But I'm not sure this is right. It quickly slips back into the tired, old, uncreative caricature of the Father as mean and grumpy and out for blood, and Jesus as the sweet, mellow pacifist who ends up dying on the cross, the victim of Daddy's anger issues.

But the New Testament writers never say the Father "poured out his wrath on the Son." Think about it: the Father wasn't angry with Jesus—Jesus was his *Son*; he was "well pleased" with Jesus.[29] Besides, what father would murder his child to get justice? The Father was angry with *evil*. And so was Jesus! Both are agonizing over the ripple effect of sin in the world. The cross was the Father and the Son *working together*, in tandem, to bring mercy and justice together—to absorb all the world's sin, and the evil it creates, in Jesus' death and release all God's life in the resurrection.[30]

Wow.

You might want to take a minute . . .

FOUR: Us

We arrive at an ending.

A bittersweet feeling, isn't it?

Let's finish like we started, with good news, but first the not so good, because it's clear by now, you're *not* a slacker.

The closing line of Exodus 34 is both hope and a warning.

The warning is this: **Yahweh will deal with sin in our lives, one way or another.** We might not take sin all that seriously, but he does. To the point of death—literally.

Sin is dehumanizing. There's no better word for it. When we sin, we become less than human; we miss the mark of all that our Creator intended for our lives. That's why God usually doesn't have to lift a finger to punish our sin. Because it is its own punishment.

For example . . .

The punishment for porn is a warped mind, an inability to see women (or men) as anything other than objects for your lust, a breach of intimacy with your spouse, and an erosion of sexual pleasure.

The punishment for lying and cheating is that eventually you get caught. You *always* get caught. And the house of cards that is your life comes apart in seconds.

The punishment for gossip is that eventually people stop trusting you, and you're left not only spiteful and angry and cynical, but alone, with a ghosting ignorance of what other people are saying about you. Paranoia becomes your regular state of mind.

And when we keep on sinning, over and over, in spite of God's mercy, eventually, we risk the hand of God against us. Trust me, you don't want God as your enemy.

The Scripture writers talk about the fear of Yahweh. This phrase is used all throughout the Bible. I cannot tell you how many times I've heard people explain it away. Saying something like, "Fear doesn't really mean fear. It means reverence or respect."

That's funny, because it says *fear*. Scripture has dozens of stories about men and women who encounter Yahweh—and in just about every story, they are *scared to death*. I mean, mop-up-the-floor-afterward afraid. Yahweh is terrifyingly good.

As the writer of Hebrews put it, "It is a fearful thing to fall into the hands of the living God."**31**

It makes me think of my childhood. I had an amazing dad. Nobody is perfect, but he was honestly incredible. But I remember the chilling line my mom would feed me when I messed up really bad: *wait until your father hears about this*. I would spend the rest of the day dreading the coming wrath. My father was never remotely abusive or violent or even mean. But he would deal with my sin. Because he saw something better in me.

As a dad now myself, I love my three kids way too much to wink at their sin. To excuse it or ignore it or sweep it under the rug. I want it *gone* from their life. I want them to grow into all that God created them to be. My job as a parent is to help them uncouple from the baggage that will hold them back from life to the full.

In the same way, Yahweh's parent-like, fatherly mercy has no end. But that doesn't mean he won't deal with your sin. If anything, it means he will take it even *more* seriously—because you're his child.

I think of the famous line in Hebrews about how "the Lord disciplines the one he loves . . . God is treating you as his children. For what children are not disciplined by their father? If you are not disciplined . . . then you are not legitimate, not true sons and daughters at all."**32**

There's a kid in our neighborhood who is a criminal mastermind-in-waiting. The next Capone. Seriously. When my kids see her, they literally run in the other direction. But I don't discipline her, mostly because it's illegal, sadly, but also because *she's not my kid*.

Occasionally, I hear people say, "God never punishes his children."

Wait, what?

Of *course* he does! Every good father does. If you're Yahweh's child, you can *expect* his discipline in your life. After all, you're loved. Deeply loved.

Maybe you need to put this book down and go repent. By "repent," I don't just mean feel guilty or lounge around in a melancholy mood for a few days; I mean genuine remorse followed by a change of lifestyle. Bring your sin straight to Jesus. Don't hide it or lie about it or make excuses for it. Just bring it right to him, and let him take it away. Absorb it on the cross. Break its hold over you in the resurrection. Set you free.

And that's the good news, the hope: **we can break free from sin, even sin that runs back for generations**. The hope of "to the third and fourth" is that we don't have to repeat the mistakes of our parents and grandparents and great-grandparents. We can get off the hamster wheel. Reclaim our humanity. We don't have to stay stuck. If you're living under the shadow of generational sin, you live in terror that you'll grow up to be like your father or mother. Listen, what was true of your parents *doesn't have to be true of you*. You can change the trajectory of your family line. Here. Now. With Jesus. You can bring your sin to Jesus, repent, and watch the handcuffs of porn or lying or gossip or greed or envy or bitterness, or *whatever* it is for you, fall off your wrists and clang to the floor.

Have you done that?

If so, you are forgiven.

Really, truly, honest-to-God forgiven.

Do you have any idea what a staggering reality that is? Your sins are *gone*. Forever. As the psalm (after quoting Exodus 34, I might add) says, "as far as the east is from the west."[33] That's a poetic way of saying that your sins are never coming back to haunt you. The slate is clean.

And if you're reading this book and you're not a follower of Jesus, not yet—well, you've made it this far. That's impressive. Really.

You ready for the next step?

You can bring all the good and bad and hope and pain and success and failure that is your life before Jesus. Here. Now. And you can give it to him, and in turn, receive mercy. You can be forgiven too.

You can become a daughter or a son with full access to the Father. With nothing standing between you relationally. All your sin gone. Over. Done. *Finito.* Nothing between you and the Maker of all.

All I can say then is: welcome to the family.

Now, to tie this off . . .

If you're thinking, *That's all great, John Mark, but I've already done that. I know I'm a daughter, a son. I know I'm right with God. But I'm still sweeping up the mess I made five years ago. A decade ago. Two decades ago. That thing you said about how we can miss out on blessing irretrievably? Yeah, I get it. That's my life.*

As followers of Jesus, we have the hope of life forever with God in a world set free from evil, and that's great, but there's a whole lot of life between now and then, and if we've made any life-altering mistakes, nobody wants to spend it moping around in regret.

Let's end with one last quote from Exodus 34. We haven't had time to look at every one of them in the Bible, but we *have* to squeeze this one in, and I can't think of a better place to do it. This one is from the prophet Joel. We don't know a lot about his book, but it's clear he writes in a time of crisis in Israel. Some kind of a disaster has swept through the country, like a plague of locusts through a field.

But Joel has a message from Yahweh:

> "Even now," declares the LORD [Yahweh],
>   "return to me with all your heart,
>   with fasting and weeping and mourning" . . .
> Return to the LORD [Yahweh] your God,
>   for he is gracious and compassionate,
>   slow to anger and abounding in love,
>   and he relents from sending calamity.
> Who knows? He may turn and relent
>   and leave behind a blessing.[34]

I love Joel's paraphrase of "forgiving wickedness, rebellion and sin. Yet he does not leave the guilty unpunished." Joel just says, "He relents from sending calamity."

And then Joel ends with a provocative question: Who knows? God could even change his mind and leave behind a blessing.

It's true that sin is incredibly cruel. And it's true that when we sin, we often lose blessing irretrievably.

But it's even *more* true that Yahweh is compassionate and gracious, slow to anger, abounding in love and faithfulness, and forgiving of every sin imaginable.

If you return . . .

If you run back to your Father . . .

If you fold yourself back into his chest . . .

Who knows?

He could turn and *naham* . . .

He could respond, with mercy . . .

In the aftermath of your sin, when the locusts have left and you're standing in the wreckage of what used to be your life, you could find your hands full of seeds for a new crop, the soil under your toes dark and rich, and maybe even feel a drop of rain on your cheek . . .

Epilogue

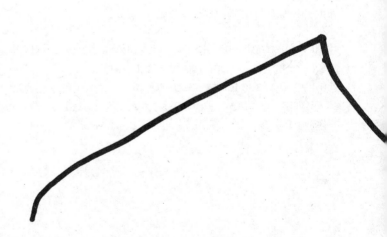

Jealous

Yesterday my six-year-old told me he's a lousy rock climber.

We were in the kitchen making dinner, and he was telling me about a birthday party on the docket for the weekend. Apparently, the birthday boy's parents rented out an entire rock climbing gym to party hard. (Making the rest of us parents look bad—thanks a lot!) It sounded like six-year-old heaven on earth to me, but *nooo*. Mo was really nervous. Scared he would climb . . . and fall.

That's when he said, "Daddy, I'm really bad at rock climbing."

Here's the thing—he's never *been* rock climbing. Not once.

But when he thinks about climbing up a twenty-foot wall with his bare hands, it's terrifying, because all he can imagine is falling back down.

Is that how you feel about the ideas in this book? About climbing up the mountain to meet Yahweh? Scared of falling? Is it intimidating? Like it's too much for a "normal" person like you?

We started this book on top of Mount Sinai, where I'm sure climbing was involved. Let's end in the same place. I want to show you what happens *next*.

After God tells Moses his name—Yahweh, the God who is compassionate and gracious and on down the list—we read this: "Moses bowed to the ground at once and worshiped."[1]

Because the only fitting, rational response to *this* kind of God is worship.

All worship is response to who Yahweh is. And by "worship," I don't just mean singing a handful of songs at church on Sunday. Worship is an entire life oriented around wonder and awe at the nature of God.

We've been saying a lot about how God *responds.*

Guess what? *So do we.*

How?

Simple: we worship.

We don't worship Yahweh to manipulate him into blessing us—to curry his favor or get on his good side. No, he's *compassionate* and *gracious*. We're *already* on his good side.

And we don't worship God to mitigate his anger, as if he's an implacable deity just waiting to lash out at the tiniest infraction. No, he's *slow to anger*.

Nor do we worship God because our life is falling apart and we need "the Man upstairs" to come through in a pinch. No, he's *abounding in love and faithfulness*.

We worship Yahweh *because he's Yahweh*.

When you see through all the myths and misconceptions about God, and Yahweh's character starts to come into view, what else could you do but worship?

So we find Moses down on his face, but he doesn't stay there. He gets back up and makes a bold, audacious request . . .

"Lord," he said, "if I have found favor in your eyes, then let the Lord go with us. Although this is a stiff-necked people, forgive our wickedness and our sin, and take us as your inheritance."

Moses is begging Yahweh to stay in relationship with Israel, even after they went off to worship the golden cows. But by now you should know Yahweh needs very little coaxing. In the next line, he responds: "I am making a covenant with you. Before all your people I will do wonders never before done in any nation in all the world."

Not only will Yahweh "go with" Israel, but they will become the stage on which his story will play out to the world. As a nation, they will become a living theater for all the nations to watch closely—to see what Yahweh is like and eventually come to worship him as well.

But then Yahweh says something out of left field: "Be careful not to make a covenant with those who live in the land where you are going, or they will be a snare among you. Break down their altars, smash their sacred stones and cut down their Asherah poles. Do not worship any other god. For the LORD [Yahweh], *whose name is Jealous*, is a jealous God."[2]

Wait, Yahweh is . . . *jealous*?

I was reading this passage to my kids before bed last night, and Jude—my nine-year-old—said, "Wait, Dad, stop. Why is God jealous? Isn't that kind of selfish? He wants Israel to worship him only or he gets mad. How is that okay?"

Great question.

God is jealous, but it's not the jealousy of a selfish boyfriend—controlling and insecure, checking his girlfriend's phone when she's out of the room. It's the jealousy of a loving, faithful, passionate husband—fighting to keep all the other lovers out of the bedroom. Of a mother fighting to keep her teenage son away from the local drug dealer.

But here's what's interesting: the text can be translated,

"whose name is Jealous"

or

"who is jealous *for his name*."

Yahweh is jealous for his reputation. In fact, people coming to see him for who he really is, is one of the central themes of the Bible. That's where we come in. Because Yahweh is locked in relationship with us, there is a symbiotic relationship between Yahweh's *name*—his reputation—and how we, the people of God, *live*.

Because Yahweh's name is also *our* name.

Throughout the Scriptures, we read that Israel is called *by the name of Yahweh*.[3] The idea here is we have an intimate, family-like relationship with the Creator—like a spouse or a child.

My wife's maiden name was Jauregui (How-ray-gee). Her grandfather was a count from the Basque Country in Spain. Sadly, she's not rich, but it's still a really cool last name. But when she became my wife, she took on a new last name: Tammy Comer. Not nearly as catchy, but much easier to say. Now she's "called by my name." So are my kids. Even my adopted daughter now shares my last name: Sunday Comer.

Are you getting the idea? As God's people, we are called by his name. But with this incredible marriage-like, family-like relationship we have with Yahweh comes a staggering responsibility to mirror and mimic what God is like to the world.

What Yahweh wants is a living, breathing people to put his name on display. To show the world what he is like, not only by what we say, but by how we *live*.

That's what Yahweh is after: a people who are "godly," who are *like* the God they worship.

A people who are compassionate . . .

A people who are gracious . . .

A people who are slow to anger . . .

A people who are abounding in love and faithfulness . . .

And a people who live in the tension of mercy and justice.

Wouldn't that really be something?

So to wrap up, let me just say it's been a pleasure to go on this journey with you.

Here's my closing word: don't be afraid to climb the mountain. Step into the smoke and fire. Devote your life to the pursuit of this terrifyingly good God.

If you fall along the way, scrape up your knees, lose ground, that's okay. Give it another go.

And remember—everywhere you set your foot, you carry the name.

You're not just a barista—you're a living, breathing example of what Yahweh is like.

You're not just a software engineer or an entrepreneur at a tech start-up—you're a temple on legs. A house of God.

You're not just a college student or a professional ballerina or a full-time parent—you're an intermediary between heaven and earth.

So as you put this book on a shelf and go about your life, remember this:

You're not just walking down to the market to pick up dinner,

you're carrying the name.

You're not just dropping by the office for a meeting,

you're carrying the name.

You're not just heading to the dog park to let Toto blow off a little steam,

you're carrying the name.

Everywhere you go . . .

In all that you do . . .

You are called by the name of Yahweh.

And it's a really good name.

Thanks

To Gerry (aka Dr. Breshears), for introducing me to Exodus 34v6–7 as quite possibly "the most quoted passage *in* the Bible, *by* the Bible," not to mention reading my teachings *every* week, answering my never-ending battery of phone calls with random theology questions, and generally being my pastor and friend.

To Dr. Tim Mackie—the only PhD I know who rides a skateboard to work—for that day in the office, drawing on a whiteboard and giving me pages of fodder for this book. And for being brilliant *and* nice.

To Bridgetown Church, elders, and staff. Love you guys so dang much. Thanks for letting me sneak away to write this thing and, above all, for "practicing the way of Jesus, together, in Portland." I still believe we're just getting started.

To Lauri Root, for giving me keys to your sweet guest house on Balboa Island. The best chapters were all written in the sun on your upstairs balcony—not surprising! California in March is heaven on earth for a Portlander. Grateful.

To the Comers, Jaureguis, our community, and all my close friends, for all the love, support, and prayer. Family is life.

To the entire crew at Zondervan: Carolyn McCready (coffee soon?!); Tom Dean—the *legend*; Dirk—you got style, sir; Jennifer; David; Curt; and all of you I don't even know about! And of course to Skye Jethani for editing this beast. Already working on the next one.

To Dave Lomas, for being a really good friend.

To T, for saying *yes* fifteen years ago. Broder Nord Friday morning?

And above all, to Yahweh, for being better than I could ever imagine.

Notes

Prologue: The God on top of the mountain

1. In his defense, he's nine, and *World War Z* is all the rage at his elementary school. And no, parents, we don't let our kids watch zombie movies. Not yet.

2. This is from the opening page of Tozer's *The Knowledge of the Holy* (1961; repr., San Francisco: Harper-SanFrancisco, 1975).

3. This is found on the same page of Tozer's book.

4. The source of this quote is in dispute. The Swiss philosopher Jean-Jacques Rousseau is the most likely, but Mark Twain frequently gets credit.

5. This is a line from Genesis 3v5. Once you get past the talking snake, this is one of the most profound and insightful stories into the human condition ever written.

6. It was Chris Martin of Coldplay. You can read a great article on his spirituality ("Coldplay's Quiet Storm" by Austin Scaggs) at www.rollingstone.com/music/news/coldplays-quiet-storm-20050825.

7. If you want to learn more about the story of God so far—in *Genesis* and *Exodus*—go to www.jointhebibleproject.com and watch Dr. Tim Mackie's videos on these books in the Torah Series and the Read Scripture Old Testament Series. One of the best things I've ever seen.

8. Exodus 33v11.

9. Exodus 33v18.

10. Raymond Ortlund Jr. said, "The glory of the Lord . . . is God himself becoming visible, God bringing his presence down to us, God displaying his beauty before us." This is from Ortlund's *Isaiah: God Saves Sinners* (Wheaton, IL: Crossway, 2005), 237. This is very different from how we use the word *glory* today, where it usually means "fame" or "credit."

11. Exodus 33v20. This entire story is from Exodus 33 and 34.

12. Exodus 33v19.

13. Exodus 34v5–7.

14. Old Testament scholar W. Ross Blackburn writes, "It is difficult to overestimate the importance of the above verses. They are the longest and most complete description of the Lord's character to be found in the Scriptures, and . . . later Scriptures frequently return to them" (*The God Who Makes Himself Known: The Missionary Heart of the Book of Exodus* [Downers Grove, IL: InterVarsity, 2012], 153).

15. I first heard this from Dr. Gerry Breshears of Western Seminary. He got it from Dr. John Sailhamer, of legendary OT scholar fame. Dr. Tim Mackie calls it "the John 3v16 of the Hebrew Bible." Here's the short list of where it's quoted: Numbers 14v18; Psalms 86v15; 103v8; 111v4; 112v4; 145v8; Jeremiah 32v18; Joel 2v13; Jonah 4v2; Nahum 1v3; Nehemiah 9v17, 31; 2 Chronicles 30v9. But what are much harder to quantify are all the allusions to it, for which I lack space in the endnotes. For example, "love and faithfulness"— first used here—is used hundreds of times in the Bible.

16. This isn't a book about the omnis, nor is it a systematic theology approach to God. There are plenty of great books out there that come at God that way. A. W. Tozer's *The Knowledge of the Holy* and J. I. Packer's *Knowing God* are great examples. The problem is, all the omnis come out of a Greek-influenced, Western way of reading the Bible. The scholastic method is negation: to decide based on observation of what is good or bad (like, say, emotions or change), and then say God has no negative attributes, so therefore he's the opposite. The problem is, these are totally Western categories, not Hebrew categories. But once again, this isn't a book about that. This is a book about the relational side of God.

17. The Babylonian Talmud (an ancient commentary on the Torah) says there are thirteen on the list, but Jewish tradition does not agree on what the thirteen actually *are*. Usually they include the next couple of paragraphs from the Exodus passage and add "jealous" to the list.

18. Exodus 3v14.

19. Exodus 33v18.

Yahweh

1. Michael Knowles, *The Unfolding Mystery of the Divine Name: The God of Sinai in Our Midst* (Downers Grove, IL: IVP Academic, 2012), 27.

2. Genesis 17v5–6.

3. Genesis 32v26.

4. Exodus 33v19, my emphasis.

5. That would be Christianity, Judaism, and Islam.

6. Genesis 17v1.

7. Genesis 14v18–19, 22.

8. Genesis 21v33.

9. Exodus 3v6.

10. See Exodus 3v13.

11. See Dr. Walter Kaiser's comments on this passage in the *Exodus* portion of *The Expositor's Commentary*, vol. 2 (Grand Rapids: Zondervan, 2008), 370–71, 373.

12. Exodus 3v15.

13. A root word is just what it sounds like—the root that other words are based off. So "love" is the root word for "lovely" and "lovable" and so on.

14. Exodus 20v7.

15. Exodus 3v15.

16. This line is from one of my all-time favorite books, A. W. Tozer's *The Pursuit of God* (Camp Hill, PA: Christian Publications, 1993), 17.

17. This is from Exodus 6v2–3.

18. In theology, this is called progressive revelation.

19. We're back again to Exodus 34v5–7.

20. John 1v14.

21. John 17v6, 26. The NIV reads "revealed *you*" and "made *you* known"—with notes at the bottom that read "*your name*." I suspect the translators did this because most modern readers don't understand the idea of meanings behind names.

22. John 17v6 MSG.

23. A lot of people reading the Bible for the first time are turned off by the language of "Father" and "he" for God. Why not "Mother"? Or "she"? To clarify, these aren't statements about God's gender, but his *nature*.

24. For a great read on how the gospel is *way* more than "going to heaven when you die," I recommend N. T. Wright's *Surprised by Hope* (San Francisco: HarperSanFrancisco, 2007) or my last book, *Garden City* (Grand Rapids: Zondervan, 2015).

25. Exodus 33v11.

26. This is, of course, my horrible millennial paraphrase of Exodus 33v12–23.

27. Dr. Breshears used to say this line all the time in class when I was in seminary. It made all of us uncomfortable, in a good way. If you want to know more, shoot Gerry an email!

28. This fascinating story is from Exodus 32. This line is from verse 14.

29. Jeremiah 18v7–10, my emphasis.

30. Barth says this in his book *The Doctrine of God: Part 1*, vol. 2 of *Church Dogmatics* (Edinburgh: T&T Clark, 1957), 496.

31. Still don't buy it? Go read Amos 7v1–6.

32. To clarify, I'm not a Calvinist, but this vision of God *is* compatible with Calvinist theology. The scholar Bruce A. Ware has a great essay on this idea of God *naham*ing. He clarifies the difference between God's "ontological and ethical immutability" and his "relational and emotional mutability." The essay appears in the *Journal of the Evangelical Theological Society* (December 1986) and is titled "An Evangelical Reformulation of the Doctrine of the Immutability of God": www.etsjets.org/files/JETS -PDFs/29/29-4/29-4-pp431-446_ JETS.pdf.

33. John 17v26, my emphasis. Where the text of the NIV reads "made *you* known," I'm using the NIV footnote's "made *your name* known."

34. This is from Dallas Willard, *The Divine Conspiracy: Rediscovering our Hidden Life in God* (San Francisco: HarperSanFrancisco, 1998), 244.

35. James 5v16.

36. In all fairness, Skye edited this book for me, and this was a comment he emailed when suggesting improvements to this chapter. I thought it was so good I just put it in! Steal . . .

37. Larry Hurtado, brilliant guy. His scholarly book on the subject is *Lord Jesus Christ* (Grand Rapids: Eerdmans, 2003). This quote is from his *At the Origins of Christian Worship* (Grand Rapids: Eerdmans, 2000), 107.

Yahweh

1. Most Hindus do not practice animal sacrifice. But many still do.

2. The famous Hindu scholar Pandurang Vaman Kane says this about karma in the Dharmasastra texts: "A good action has its reward and a bad action leads to retribution. If the bad actions do not yield their consequences in this life, the soul begins another existence and in the new environment undergoes suffering for its past deeds." This quote is in the "Dharmasastra" article in the *World Heritage Encyclopedia*, www.worldlibrary.org/articles/dharmasastra.

3. Of course, India is moving in the right direction with laws to protect the Dalit from discrimination, but ancient traditions don't die quickly.

4. If you want to know more or maybe even go visit, head to hearthecry.org or indiahappyhome.org.

5. From Mark 1v15.

6. Honestly, there are a number of theories on why his name is repeated, and nobody knows for sure. The most likely is it has to do with his desire to be in relationship with Israel. But for sure he's driving home the idea of his name.

7. This is mostly true of the Old Testament, where he's usually called "the LORD God." In the New Testament, which was written in Greek, this changes a bit.

8. In fact, *elohim* can be translated singular or plural, depending on the context. So when you read "God" and when you read "the gods," you're actually reading a translation of the exact same Hebrew word. In Genesis 1v1, we know "God" is the right translation because the verb "create" is singular, and in Hebrew, the subject and verb always agree.

9. Of course, we have no way of knowing when Genesis 1 was written, much less when it happened. It was probably around as an oral tradition for centuries before Moses (or whoever) ever wrote it down.

10. Exodus 12v12.

11. There's a great article by Ziony Zevit in *Bible Review* (June 1990) called "Exodus in the Bible and the Egyptian Plagues." You can find it at www.biblicalarchaeology.org/daily/biblical-topics/exodus/exodus-in-the-bible-and-the-egyptian-plagues.

12. This is in Exodus 10v21–29. Technically, it's the second-to-last plague. The last one is the death of the firstborn. But that has to do with Pharaoh—who was also seen as a god in human flesh.

13. Numbers 33v4.

14. This would be Jethro, Moses' father-in-law, in Exodus 18v11.

15. Exodus 15v11. Read the entire poem, especially the first couple of verses. It's striking.

16. Psalms 86v8; 96v4; 97v7, 9. My emphasis added in all these examples.

17. Exodus 20v3. The phrase "before me" can also be translated "above me" or "in place of me."

18. I honestly mean that. I work hard to read the Old Testament in its ancient Near Eastern context. It could be that God is just speaking to Israel in a language they understand, accommodating their incorrect worldview of many "gods" and giving them time to catch up to the idea of *one* God. But I don't think so. I think there's some truth to their worldview that continues well into the New Testament. You'll have to judge for yourself.

19. The story is told in Exodus 7–12.

20. Deuteronomy 6v4.

21. 1 Kings 11v2, 4, my emphasis.

22. 1 Kings 11v5, 7.

23. This is in Daniel 10v13.

24. Daniel 10v20.

25. Here's the tragic list: http://en.wikipedia.org/wiki/List_of_shootings_in_Colorado.

26. See also 1 Kings 22v19–23; Amos 7v1–9; Job 1–2; Psalms 29v1; 82v6; 89v7; Jeremiah 23v16–22.

27. See the ESV and NRSV.

28. Psalm 89v5–8 is another great example. Go read it. It's pretty crazy.

29. This is from Aaron Chalmer's book *Interpreting the Prophets* (Downers Grove, IL: InterVarsity, 2015), 12.

30. Psalm 82v2–4.

31. To be in the clear, there is a legitimate alternate interpretation to the one I'm giving. There's one place, in Exodus 22v7–9, where almost everybody translates *elohim* as "judges," and human judges seem to be in view. That could be the meaning here, but I really don't think so, because the divine council language doesn't make sense. Plus, Jesus quotes Psalm 82v6 in John 10v34. It's a notoriously difficult passage to interpret as well, but as I see it, to read the *elohim* as human judges seems to make Jesus' entire point nonsensical. It makes it sound like he's backing away from his claims to be the embodiment of God. It seems much more likely that Jesus is quoting Psalm 82—a well-known poem about the "gods"—and using it to bolster his argument: if these rotten spiritual beings are called "gods," why is it so unthinkable that Jesus himself would be called the "Son of God." I think he's trying to help his critics see the beauty of God coming into the world as a human being.

32. Psalm 82v6–7.

33. That would be the legendary Dr. Gerry Breshears.

34. This is Isaiah 45v5, my emphasis.

35. I like the NET Bible's translation the best: "I am the Lord, I have no peer, there is no God but me."

36. 1 Corinthians 8v5, my emphasis.

37. In Deuteronomy 32v12 (which, by the way, is a fascinating passage on how the nations were given over to the "gods") and Psalm 106v37.

38. Unless you count the cherubim in Isaiah 6. But they definitely aren't Swedish!

39. Thank goodness for *Rogue One*, which, for the record, is one of the best Star Wars films ever.

40. 1 John 3v8 in the NLT, my emphasis.

41. Acts 10v38, my emphasis.

42. Mark 1v39, my emphasis.

43. Colossians 2v15.

44. For a *great* book on the multifaceted nature of the atonement, pick up *The Cross of Christ* by John

Stott (Downers Grove, IL: InterVarsity, 1986). And if you want to know even more about *Christus Victor*, start with Greg Boyd's work on it in his chapter in *The Nature of the Atonement: Four Views*, ed. James K. Beilby and Paul R. Eddy (Downers Grove, IL: InterVarsity, 2006). Yup, John Stott and Greg Boyd in one sentence. I think they would have gotten along.

45. Of course, there are multiple types of "universalism." There are ancient forms of universalism that see salvation for *all* people, even those who don't follow Jesus. That's not a new idea—but the idea of "all paths [read, religions] lead to God" is relatively new.

46. This is in Ephesians 3v10.

47. Look at 1 Corinthians 1v3, Galatians 1v3, Ephesians 1v2, and Philippians 1v2 for examples.

48. The book of Job is the closest thing, but it's really more about God's justice than the question of evil. When you read the New Testament, *not one* of the authors is wrestling with the problem of evil.

49. Read this in Matthew 6v10.

50. If you want to know more of my thoughts on this thorny topic, feel free to listen to a series I did on the problem of evil: http://bridgetown.church/teaching.

51. Greg Boyd in *God at War* (Downers Grove, IL: InterVarsity, 1997), 129, my emphasis. This is one of the best books I've ever read. Even if you hate his open theism stuff, it's still a really helpful read. To clarify, I'm *not* an open theist, but I think the mild version that Boyd advocates does have some great things to say and needs to be given a fair hearing, even if you simply chew the meat and spit out the bones.

52. For more information on how secularism created the problem of evil in its current form, read *Walking with God through Pain and Suffering* by Tim Keller (New York: Dutton, 2013). He does a great job of pointing to the Lisbon earthquake of 1755 as the turning point in Western's thinking on evil.

53. 1 Corinthians 10v14.

54. 1 John 5v21. This is actually one of the last things John wrote as an elderly man—his final warning to his church.

55. This is from Tim Keller's book *Counterfeit Gods* (New York: Dutton, 2009), xix, 155. I'm a huge Keller fan, even if I disagree on this point.

56. This is in 1 Corinthians 10v19–20, my emphasis.

57. This is found in Wright's *Evil and the Justice of God* (Downers Grove, IL: InterVarsity, 2011), 112.

58. The quote is actually a paraphrase from the French poet Charles Baudelaire; it's found in the classic 1995 film *The Usual Suspects*.

59. His commencement speech was put into a great little book called *This Is Water* (New York: Little, Brown, 2009). Takes about fifteen minutes to read, and it is just fantastic.

Compassionate and gracious

1. Dates vary, but probably between 1260 and 1240 BC. A few hundred years after the exodus.

2. Some versions say because of the young men who were about to die in battle (see Aeschylus's play *Agamemnon*), others because Agamemnon killed an animal sacred to Artemis and bragged that he was her equal in hunting (see Sophocles's *Electra*).

3. For a fascinating (and disturbing) biblical example of this, go read 2 Kings 3v26–27. The story is vague, but it seems to connect the king of Moab's sacrificing of his firstborn son to an unnamed deity to Moab's victory over Israel.

4. Note that in the Hebrew, the word *hanun* has *we* attached to it—that's the conjunction "and."

5. In fact, in the ESV, it's "merciful" in Exodus 34v6.

6. This is in 1 Kings 3v26.

7. Isaiah 49v15, my emphasis.

8. Psalm 103v8, 13, my emphasis.

9. This is Exodus 22v26–27 (my emphasis), but I had to mix two translations. All except the last word is from the NIV, but I've substituted "gracious" (from the NASB) instead of "compassionate." It's a bit confusing, because *hanun* is often translated "compassionate" as well. Hence, my mutt translation.

10. 2 Kings 13v22–23, my emphasis.

11. This is Psalm 86v15–16, but, once again, I had to mix translations. Verse 15 is from the NIV, and v16 is from the ESV.

12. This choice quote is from Ashurnasirpal II.

13. This and the preceding two quotes are found in Daniel David Luckenbill's *Ancient Records of Assyria and Babylon*, 2 vols. (Chicago: University of Chicago Press, 1926), 1:213, 1:146, 2:319.

14. Jonah 1v3.

15. Which, by the way, is a real place. In Mali.

16. For those of you skeptics like myself who have a really hard time with the "big fish" story, there is good reason to believe that Jonah isn't an autobiography. That it's more like historical fiction. Jonah was real, and Assyria was real, but it's the only prophetic book in the Bible that doesn't start with a marker for its date and time (usually they start by saying the year of the king). Plus, it's chock-full of hyperbolic language. My Hebrew professor called it "an ancient Jewish comic book." Personally, I learn toward that view, but I'm fine with either.

17. Jonah 3v4.

18. This is in Jonah 3v10.

19. Once again, "changed his mind" is an English phrase, not a Hebrew one, and you could easily get the wrong idea. I'm not questioning Yahweh's omniscience or saying he changed his *knowledge*. Rather, it seems that he changed his *attitude* or *relationship* toward Nineveh. Once again, see Bruce Ware's in-depth explanation: www.etsjets.org/files/JETS-PDFs/29/29-4/29-4-pp431-446_JETS.pdf.

20. Jonah 4v2–3, my emphasis.

21. This is from the Sermon on the Mount in Matthew 5v43–44.

22. Matthew 5v45.

23. The New Testament was written in Greek, not Hebrew. So figuring out when the writers are quoting Exodus 34 can be a bit tricky. Here's how I did it: a few hundred years before Jesus, the Hebrew Bible was translated into Greek in a version called the Septuagint. It was the popular Bible of Jesus' day and was used by all the New Testament authors to quote the Old Testament. So I just used the Septuagint's translation of Exodus 34 as my base.

24. This is from Luke 17v13 in the ESV, my emphasis. The Septuagint scholars translated "compassionate and gracious" in Exodus 34v6 as *eleos*, the word I'm using here.

25. Luke 18v38, my emphasis.

26. Matthew 17v15, my emphasis.

27. The story is told in Luke 15v11–32.

28. Luke 15v13.

29. Luke 15v20, my emphasis.

30. Matthew 5v44–45, my emphasis.

31. Luke 6v36.

32. Romans 12v6, 8.

33. Hebrews 4v16, my emphasis.

Slow to anger

1. In scholarship, the correct terms are "formal equivalence" and "dynamic equivalence." Formal equivalence works harder to mimic the exact wording of the original text, whereas dynamic equivalence thinks the best way to translate is to change the wording to better convey the original thought. It's not better/worse, but a genuine philosophical disagreement. For example, if you wanted to translate *Cuántos años tienes usted?* from Spanish into English, a formal equivalence translation would be, "How many years have you?" but a dynamic equivalence translation would be "How old are you?" Which one is the "best" translation? Hard to say. Hence, the debate goes on . . .

2. Proverbs 14v29. The NIV translates *erek apayim* as "patient."

3. Proverbs 16v32 in the ESV.

4. This is from the Aramaic *Targum Neofiti 1: Exodus* (Collegeville, MN: Liturgical Press, 1994), 138.

5. This is in Psalm 7v11–12, my emphasis.

6. Habakkuk 3v2, my emphasis.

7. Psalm 5v5–6, my emphasis.

8. Psalm 11v5, my emphasis.

9. This is from John Stott's masterful book *The Cross of Christ*, 20th anniv. ed. (Downers Grove, IL: InterVarsity, 2012), 171.

10. This is found in Cornelius Plantinga Jr.'s *Not the Way It's Supposed* *to Be* (Grand Rapids: Eerdmans, 1996), 58.

11. Exodus 21v24.

12. From the 2008 film *Taken*.

13. This is all from Nahum 1v2–3, my emphasis.

14. Here are three examples where the phrase or concept is used: Genesis 15v16, Matthew 23v32, and 1 Thessalonians 2v16.

15. Just a few years later, in 612 BC.

16. He wrote this in "A Contribution to the Critique of Hegel's Philosophy of Right," an essay in *Deutsch-Französische Jahrbücher* in 1844.

17. This is found in his essay titled "The Discreet Charm of Nihilism" in *New York Review of Books*, November 19, 1998.

18. 2 Samuel 6v7.

19. The second inaugural address is found at http://avalon.law.yale.edu/19th_century/lincoln2.asp.

20. You can read this in Romans 1v24, 26, 28, my emphasis.

21. This is not true for those who love and follow Jesus in the Spirit. Your deepest desires are from the Spirit. I'm talking about people whose hearts are out of sync with Yahweh's.

22. As Job said it, "Why do the wicked live, reach old age, and grow mighty in power?" (Job 21v7 in the ESV).

23. Psalms 6v3 and 13v1, for example.

24. This is found in a *U.S. News & World Report* interview ("Humankind: Wisdom, Philosophy, and Other Musings," p. 86), October 27, 1986.

25. Mark 1v15.

26. For a great book on the gospel, read *The King Jesus Gospel* by Scot McKnight (Grand Rapids: Zondervan, 2016). He does a great job challenging the many misconceptions about the gospel and calling us to rethink the basic message of Jesus.

27. This requirement is found in many places in the Torah, including Exodus 12v5, Leviticus 1v3, and Numbers 6v14.

28. This is from John 2v13–17. It shows up in all four Gospels. Whenever that happens, we take notice. It's like Matthew, Mark, Luke, and John all got together and said, "People *need* to know this."

29. My theory on hipsters' obsession with flannel is that it all goes back to Sunday school . . .

30. Some scholars disagree and think this happened earlier, because in John's gospel, it's in chapter 2. But most scholars argue that John's gospel isn't in chronological order, and that the other three Gospels put it at the end because it was one of the main reasons Jesus was arrested and crucified.

31. 1 John 4v8.

32. I was first exposed to this idea that "how we relate is how we relate" in a book called *The Relational Soul* by Richard Plass and James Cofield (Downers Grove, IL: InterVarsity, 2014). Can't recommend it enough, especially if you're dealing with wounds from your family of origin.

33. It's called *The Emotionally Healthy Church* by Peter Scazzero (updated edition was published by Zondervan in 2015), and it's *fantastic*.

34. This is James 1v19–20, my emphasis.

35. From chapter 5v7, 8, 10, my emphasis. The word James uses in Greek for the idea of patience is *makrothymia*, and it's the Greek translation of *erek apayim*, or "slow to anger."

36. This is from chapter 5v11, my emphasis.

37. James 5v9.

Abounding in love and faithfulness

1. If you want to know more, I have a book all about this. It's called *Loveology*. Yes, this is a shameless plug.

2. Daniel Block, *Judges, Ruth* (Nashville: Broadman & Holman, 1999), 634–35.

3. Psalm 89v1–2, my emphasis.

4. Psalm 89v28, 33, my emphasis.

5. This is in Genesis 12v2–3.

6. Read Genesis 17v1–8 for the story on Abram's name change.

7. This is in Genesis 15v12–17.

8. Nehemiah 9v17, my emphasis.

9. Nehemiah 9v32–33, my emphasis.

10. Acts 3v25–26.

11. That's why Paul calls Genesis 12 the "gospel in advance" in Galatians 3v8.

12. 2 Timothy 2v13.

13. John 16v33.

14. Matthew 6v10. Read also Luke 22v42.

15. Romans 8v28. Please note that this line is usually misquoted as "all things work together for good." It does *not* say that.

16. Isaiah 54v2–3.

17. This is in Proverbs 22v6 in the KJV.

18. Read the report issued by the U.S. Census Bureau in 2011 for "Number, Timing, and Duration of Marriages and Divorces: 2009," 15, 18. It's found at www.census.gov/prod/2011pubs/p70-125.pdf.

19. 4.4, to be exact. See the *Forbes* article by Jeanne Meister: www.forbes.com/sites/jeanne meister/2012/08/14/job-hopping -is-the-new-normal-for-millennials -three-ways-to-prevent-a-human -resource-nightmare.

20. The phrase "a long obedience in the same direction" comes, oddly enough, from Friedrich Nietzsche in his book *Beyond Good and Evil*.

Yet he does not leave the guilty unpunished

1. For example, think of his teaching in Matthew 5v17–19: "Do not think that I have come to abolish the Law or the Prophets; I have not come to abolish them but to fulfill them. For truly I tell you, until heaven and earth disappear, not the smallest letter, not the least stroke of a pen, will by any means disappear from the Law until everything is accomplished. There-fore anyone who sets aside one of the least of these commands and teaches others accordingly will be called least in the kingdom of heaven, but whoever practices and teaches these commands will be called great in the kingdom of heaven."

2. Psalm 40v11, my emphasis.

3. John 1v29, my emphasis.

4. Micah 7v18–20, my emphasis. Extra: the prophet Micah's name means "Who is like Yahweh?" and the closing paragraph in his book starts with the question "Who is a God like you?" Nice play on words from a literary prophet.

5. That would be Douglas K. Stuart,

in his commentary on *Exodus* (Nashville: Broadman & Holman, 2006), 716.

6. Once again, the ESV to the rescue. The problem is the word *guilty* isn't there in Hebrew. Just a verb meaning "to leave unpunished."

7. This is found in Romans 3v23.

8. Amos 5v24.

9. Deuteronomy 24v16, my emphasis.

10. This is Jeremiah 32v18–19, my emphasis.

11. My friend Dr. Tim Mackie first pointed this out to me, and helpful discussions can be found in good commentaries on *Exodus*, such as Doug Stuart's (Nashville: Broadman & Holman, 2006) and Umberto Cassuto's (Jerusalem: Hebrew University Magnus Press, 1967).

12. This is from James 2v13.

13. This is a common phrase in the first five books of the Bible: Exodus 3v8, 17; 13v5; 33v3; Leviticus 20v24; Numbers 13v27; 14v8; 16v13, 14; Deuteronomy 6v3; 11v9; 26v9, 15; 27v3; 31v20. The leading theory is that "milk" means it was a good land for raising livestock, and

"honey" means it was also good for agriculture. So, a rich, fertile land of opportunity.

14. This is from Numbers 14v4.

15. Numbers 14v10.

16. Genesis 2v17.

17. This is found in Genesis 3v4–5.

18. I did a series a while back on the Bible called "It Is Written" where I get into the Bible as literature and Scripture and how to read passages like Genesis 3. Feel free to listen at http://bridgetown.church/series/it-is-written.

19. Numbers 14v11–12.

20. Numbers 14v13.

21. Numbers 14v17–19, my emphasis.

22. Numbers 14v21, 23, 31–33, my emphasis.

23. John 1v14.

24. John 1v29.

25. See Hebrews 9v13 and 10v4.

26. It comes as no surprise that Jesus dies during the Jewish Feast of Passover—on the same night when the Passover lamb was killed. That's not random or accidental. The entire scene is pregnant with symbolism. Jesus frames his death around Passover. He is *the* Passover lamb—here to die in Israel's place so they can walk out of slavery into freedom.

27. Romans 3v25–26, my emphasis.

28. As Old Testament scholar Chris Wright, speaking of Exodus 34v6–7, said, "The paradox inherent in this self-description, that Yahweh is characterized by compassion, grace, love and faithfulness, and yet does not let sin go unpunished, is only finally resolved on the cross." This is from his essay, "Atonement in the Old Testament," in *The Atonement Debate*, ed. Derek Tidball et al. (Grand Rapids: Zondervan, 2008), 75.

29. Matthew 3v17.

30. For a great example of this, read Genesis 22. Abraham doesn't "pour out his wrath" on Isaac. He loves Isaac deeply, but is willing to make the ultimate sacrifice. Thankfully, Abraham didn't have to. But Yahweh did.

31. Hebrews 10v31 in the ESV.

32. See the rest in Hebrews 12v4–13.

33. Psalm 103v12.

34. This is from Joel 2v12–14.

Epilogue: Jealous

1. This is Exodus 34v8, and the rest of the story comes from the next few paragraphs in that chapter.

2. Exodus 34v12–14, my emphasis.

3. Here are a few great examples: Deuteronomy 28v10, 2 Chronicles 7v14, and Isaiah 43v7.

John Mark Comer lives, works, and writes in the urban core of Portland, Oregon, with his wife, Tammy, and their three children, Jude, Moses, and Sunday.

He is the pastor for teaching and vision at Bridgetown Church and has a master's degree in biblical and theological studies from Western Seminary. John Mark is also the author of *My Name Is Hope*, *Loveology*, and *Garden City*.

For more of John Mark's teachings on the Scriptures, Jesus, and life, go to *Bridgetown.church* and sign up for the podcast or visit *johnmarkcomer.com*.

Loveology

God. Love. Marriage. Sex. And the Never-Ending Story of Male and Female.

John Mark Comer

In the beginning, God created Adam. Then he made Eve.

And ever since we've been picking up the pieces.

Loveology is just that—a theology of love.

With an autobiographical thread that turns a book into a story, John Mark Comer shares about what is right in male/female relationships—what God intended in the Garden. And about what is wrong—the fallout in a post-Eden world.

Loveology starts with marriage and works backward. It deals with sexuality, romance, singleness, and what it means to be male and female—and ends with a raw, uncut, anything-goes Q and A that takes on the most-asked questions about sexuality and relationships.

This is a book for singles, engaged couples, and the newly married—both inside and outside the church—who want to learn what the Scriptures have to say about sexuality and relationships. For those who are tired of both Hollywood's propaganda and the church's silence. And for people who want to ask the why questions and get intelligent, nuanced, grace-and-truth answers rooted in the Scriptures.

Garden City

Work, Rest, and the Art of Being Human.

John Mark Comer

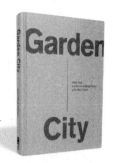

We'll all heard it said, "It's who you are that matters, not what you do."
Really?
Where do the Scriptures teach *that*?
After all, from the first page of the Bible forward, human beings were made to rule over the earth, to gather up the raw materials of planet Earth and carve out a world.

Theologically rich, yet down-to-earth and practical, *Garden City* speaks to all of us who are searching for our calling in life or just trying to find meaning in the everyday. In the end, this book is an invitation to ask the ancient, primal *human* question: Why am I here and what should I do about it?